House of Earth

A complete handbook for earthen construction

Cob
Straw-clay
Adobe
Earthbags
Plasters
Floors
Paints

By Conrad Rogue

A House Alive publication

All illustrations by Shannon Wells, John Hutton and Coenraad Rogmans.

ISBN-13: 978-1530642816

This is a House Alive publication.

"Going home
without my sorrow
Going home
sometime tomorrow
Going home
to where it's better than before..."

Leonard Cohen

Table of contents

This may be helpful...

Before you start...

There are a few things I want to share with you, before you start learning about how to build a house of earth.

I have tried to write a book without "filler". There are not too many side stories and every time something is done in a few steps, I have given it bullet points, hopefully making it easy to follow for you. All the contents reflect what I teach in workshops.

The techniques shared are about what I have found to be the most practical for housing ourselves and the world. However, I don't claim to have the "right" way of building with earth. It's also OK to do things that are not totally practical.

You can go to the companion website (www.HouseAlive.org) to get great visualizations of the things you are reading about. I try not to waste your time by keeping videos short, sweet and of good quality.

Reading this book can in no way, shape or form be a replacement for hands-on learning. It is meant to support hands-on learning. If you want to learn how to build, you have to build! The more you build, the more you learn.

The future of our planet and the life it sustains is not looking very bright right now. It is hard to imagine that this will get any better without changing the way we build houses and live in them. Considering the challenges our eco-systems and communities face, I think earth is the building material by choice for most climates and situations.

Thank you: Shannon and John for giving me some beautiful illustrations.

My students, probably more than a thousand at the time of this writing, thank you for your interest, your care, your questions, your laughter, your encouragement and your love. You have been part of this more than you may realize. Not everything always works, but let's keep throwing mud at the wall... At some point something will stick! You bring hope to this world.

James, I sometimes feel like this is as much your work as it is mine. Our many years or working together have been incredible. All our travels, building adventures, aimless discussion and beautiful workshops that we have taught together have helped me enjoy life to the fullest. So, here it is again: thank you...

Courtney, Jules and Rosie, our family came to be and grew up in an earthen house. I cannot help but thinking that you all turned so beautifully, perhaps just a little bit because of the way we lived. Thank you for all your support and love and for this amazing journey we have had together!

Oh Earth, what a beautiful building material you have given us!

Part 1:
Putting the materials, the tools and the philosophy together

House of earth...

During the dust bowl years of the 1930s, many poor people in Texas and the surrounding states lived in houses with walls made out of planks. Gaps in the wood allowed wind and dust to enter the house, and termites would slowly but surely devour the planks. It was cold in the winter, hot in the summer, and all around a miserable way to house yourself.

When singer/songwriter Woody Guthrie traveled through the Southwest, he came across houses made out of adobe block. He quickly realized that the clay-soil material for the blocks was free. All you needed was time and a few simple tools, and you could raise some walls that would be far superior to the plank houses.

Inspired by this way of building, in 1937 he decided to write a novel about it. It tells the story of a couple living in the Texas panhandle, suffering through the dust storms. They found hope in a pamphlet they purchased for five cents from the U.S. Department of Agriculture called Adobe or sun dried brick for farm buildings (USDA Farm Bulletin #1720).

To them an earthen house seemed too good to be true. Here is Tike, the main character in the book, explaining why a house of earth would be so great:

"Because the earth is so strong that it will stand for two hundred years. Because it has walls eighteen inches thick. Because it is warm in the winter, cool in the summer. Because it is easy to build and does not require any great skill to build it. Because it does not eat nickels and drink dollars, and because it needs no paint, because you don't have to work your heart and soul away and carry every penny into town to lay on the top of Mister Woodridge's desk. Because of this. Because of all these things. Because your house could be six rooms instead of these eighteen feet of disease. Because you could pay out the earth house in a year or two and it would belong to you. Because it would not belong to them. After all these years they are still bleeding people for rent, payments, this kind, that kind, on these rusted out, rotted down, firetrap wood skeletons."

In the book we never find out if the main characters end up with a "house of earth." Even though they had access to information through the bulletin, they still needed access to land, no small obstacle. The novel was finished in 1947 but was not published until 2013, edited by Douglas Brinkley and Johnny Depp.

Although the circumstances during the dust bowl were particularly rough, it is fair to say that to this day, billions of people have difficulty housing themselves with dignity. By this I mean a house that:

- is comfortable and spacious (not palatial)
- is aesthetically pleasing
- is devoid of carcinogenic toxins
- treads lightly on the world's ecosystems
- is easy and affordable to maintain
- can be paid for within a few years

Although this may seem like an idealistic list of criteria, earthen construction can effectively address most of these issues. It is with this in mind that I share my experiences from 15 years of building with earth.

Building with earth can be considered the mother of all construction techniques. It is one of the most ancient ways of building. In Eastern Europe, earthen buildings have been excavated that date back 8,000 years. The Great Wall of China, constructed 2,000 years ago, contains 400 million cubic yards of earth in the form of adobe block. Some of the great pyramids in Egypt were built in part with earth. Until the mid-20th century, when the draw of the cities and the use of concrete and steel made it less popular, it was the dominant form of construction worldwide.

Of course, this should not be surprising. Clay-soil, the main ingredient, can be found almost anywhere, and is very easy to work with. It is also interesting to note that worldwide and over the course of history, the techniques used for building with clay-soil have remained very similar. Sure, local innovations evolve, hybrid methods are developed, and new tools and hardware become available. Still, seeing someone build with earth in Yemen, which has a 1,500 year tradition of earthen building, has an overwhelming resemblance to people in Oregon building with cob.

This handbook describes the most common ways of building with earth. I have tried to focus on describing techniques that are the easiest and most straightforward, have stood the test of time, and are applicable to all but the coldest climates. These are the techniques that I have taught in my workshops with House Alive for the past 15 years. One of my hopes is that people start considering earthen construction for more than just building new houses. It is equally applicable for remodels, renovations, outdoor structures, garden walls, fireplaces, and pizza ovens.

How to use this book? It is best to read Part One in its entirety. It gives an overview of the different techniques and explains how to find and prepare materials. Part Two contains practical, step-by-step instructions for the different techniques: cob, straw-clay plaster, block building, earthbag construction, light straw-clay, earthen plasters, earthen floors, and earthen paints.

Through building with earth and contact with the clay-soil, we are doing something that humans have done for millennia. I cannot help but imagine that the joy my students find in this universal and timeless way of building is in part due to this connection with people all over the world today and throughout history.

So get muddy!
Coenraad

1.1 Why Build With Earth?

I have a house made of earth! I took the soil from beneath my feet, mixed it with water, straw, and sand, and turned it into building materials for a foundation, structural walls, insulation, finish plaster, and the floor. I also have a fireplace, interior walls, an outdoor oven, storage cubbies, bookshelves, and benches made with earth. I paint with earth, I sculpt with earth, I live with earth.

It's very empowering to learn these techniques. Suddenly you will be able to house yourself and create your own custom-built environment. It's not very hard either. If you can tie your shoes, bake a cake, and carry a small child, you can learn how to build with earth! You also have to be willing to get a little muddy, but that may just add to the appeal.

I often give tours of my house. Whenever people walk in for the first time, they always say one of three things:

• Wow!
• I could live here!
• This is beautiful!

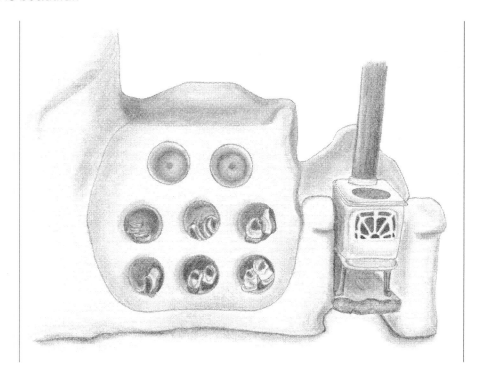

Then they feel the walls with their hands. This happens every time. I think they are experiencing a deep sense of relief and a strong feeling of "homecoming." These feelings are associated with connection and belonging to nature, the earth, history, and people.

So what's the attraction?

- The structures are beautiful. They make us feel like we are a part of nature. The absence of hard angles and dull flat surfaces makes the space feel alive. Without any need for gallery art, every section of a wall is lovely to look at.
- The construction methods are easy to learn, fun to do, safe, and easy on your body. You don't need to be super strong or technical. Everyone can help, from kids to grandma!
- The materials are free or very inexpensive. Gather them with care from your local area. There is no need to mine distant nations or clear-cut a forest.
- Earth is safe to build with and safe to live in. There are no toxic glues, paints, vinyls, or other materials that off-gas. Your house does not have to make you sick!
- It's simple to mix and match different earthen building techniques with each other as well as with conventional methods of building. Renovations become much easier. Recycled windows, doors, beams, etc. can be integrated seamlessly.
- Besides the fact that you are working with local materials, these techniques are easy on the environment in four ways: (1) During the construction process there is very little need for energy input, and there is no waste. (2) Earthen buildings are very energy efficient and easy to maintain during the life of the building. (3) Because the material is so pleasant to be with and so easy to customize, earthen buildings can be designed much smaller than those houses that are planning on using industrial materials. (4) When the life of a building is over, it can go back to the earth where it came from.
- Earthen buildings are very comfortable. They are quiet, the temperature fluctuations are gentle, and the humidity is moderated by the clay in the material. Earthen houses instill a feeling of peace and safety.
- Working with earth, we feel connected to the mother of all construction materials. Humans have continuously built with earth for at least 8,000 years; it is still practiced today by about one quarter of the world's population.
- Building with earth has the potential to create a paradigm shift: from debt ridden to mortgage free, from unable to able, from sick to healthy, from feeling lonely to becoming part of a community, from lost to grounded.

This may be helpful…

Earth as the portal to becoming mortgage free

Many people think of, and read about, building with earth as a way to quit their job, live mortgage free, and lead a simple fulfilling life, surrounded by beauty and community. This actually has happened to people and it can happen to you as well! However, it is a mistake to think that this will happen because your walls are built with earth, which you can dig up for free, right where you are building. The affordability and abundance of clay-soil will not enable you to quit your job and give up your mortgage. The question then becomes: what does?

There is no question that building with earth can lead to some immediate cost savings. This can be a result of more efficient design, built-in furniture, and the use of recycled and found materials. However, many of these savings can also be realized with more conventional construction methods. Building with earth can actually become more expensive than conventional construction, maybe because it tends to be more labor intensive and needs a stronger foundation and greater roof overhangs.

The way that earthen construction helps us to free ourselves from working jobs to pay for things we do not want is through the lessons that it teaches us. Building with earth, if we allow it, can bring about a mental shift, a change in attitude, a different outlook on life, which can be the start of unshackling ourselves from the job market and the financial industry (a.k.a. "the rat race"). Said differently, building with earth has the potential to become a portal to a different way of life through the lessons we can learn from the quality of the material and the way we use and build with it. Here are some of those lessons:

I am capable. Building with earth gives people a sense of empowerment and confidence. Feeling that you can be an "owner-builder" comes with a sense of security: "I can provide my own shelter using readily available materials."

I don't have to be alone. A fun, well-organized building site has the potential to encourage friends and neighbors to join in. People get a glimpse of what it must feel like to work together as a community, reminiscent of a barn raising or a Habitat for Humanity project.

There is enough. The supply of building materials seems to be unlimited. The clay soil is so abundant. The materials lend themselves perfectly for integrating recycled and reclaimed materials out of the waste stream, which in many parts of the world also seem unlimited.

I can make something out of nothing. By "reshaping" the earth around us into buildings, we find that we are part of a regenerative process. We have created something beautiful in the world without having taken much from it.

Enjoying my time makes life better. Often we believe that "work" is inherently unpleasant, something we do only to "get things done." Under the right circumstances people working with earth get into a flow of building that feels rewarding, beautiful, and enjoyable. Work starts to look a little more like play.

Being outside makes me feel good. During the building process, awareness may arise that we are actually meant to be outside, with the home becoming more of a place of shelter, warmth, intimacy and rest. The outside world becomes as much of a place of comfort as the inside world.

<u>I can be healthy and active.</u> A constant but gentle physical activity allows our bodies to start performing at a more optimum level, which improves our physical and mental health.

<u>Building relationships and friendships gives more security and freedom than amassing property and wealth.</u> This concept would seem like a no-brainer, but it is being fought tooth-and-nail by all aspects of our consumption-based society, in particular our schools, media, and government. Material goods can bring joy and contentment, but without community to enjoy them with, they become meaningless.

<u>A house should be a home, not an investment.</u> At this moment in time, building with earth often is a conscious choice of separating oneself from the world of housing speculation and investment. Resale value becomes unimportant, allowing us to express ourselves and satisfy our true and authentic living needs for our homes.

<u>Less is more, in so many ways.</u> Less house means less cleaning, heating, paying, and maintaining. It also means more free time, more time spent outdoors, and more vitality.

These are the lessons that building with earth generously provides to us. As people explore building with earth, they subconsciously discover these lessons which naturally helps them move in a new direction in the their lives.

1.2 The Earthen Building Techniques

Visit www.HouseAlive.org *for pictures and videos on this chapter.*

Below are descriptions of eight earthen building techniques that have been widely used over the course of history and are still practiced today worldwide. They all use earth as a basic building material and then add some combination of sand and straw to make it stronger, long lasting and beautiful. Once you understand how this works, you will be able to build just about anything out of earth.

Child playing on a cob pool table...

When we say earth, we are really talking about soil that contains some percentage of clay, from here on referred to as "Clay-soil". It is really the clay in the soil that makes all of these techniques possible. Clay-soil is almost everywhere. If you took all the clay on earth and wrapped it around the planet (like peanut butter around an apple), it would be a mile thick! You very likely have clay-soil in your backyard, in the park across the street, or in the hills nearby.

The reason why clay-soil works so well for construction is because it becomes sticky when wet. The clay molecules absorb water, swell, and stick to one another, as well as to everything surrounding them. When the clay dries, it shrinks again and may crack. Dry clay can be brittle because it does not have much structural strength. This is in part why we add sand and/or straw to the mix. Sand functions like tiny rocks, giving structure to the whole. Straw provides tensile strength; adding straw makes it harder to pull apart the material.

Before we take a closer look at these ingredients and how they work, let's review these different time-tested techniques.

Cob

Cob is a mixture of sand, straw, clay-soil, and water. Usually the mixing happens using our feet with the materials put on a small tarp on the ground, although there are many other ways to mix as well. Once it is mixed to a sticky, dough-like consistency, the material is put directly on the wall. As the wall goes up, the preceding layers dry while new wet material is added on top. Saws, machetes, and levels are used to keep the walls straight. Because it is applied in a wet, pliable form, it easily lends itself to unique and rounded shapes (no forms required), including arches, niches, bookshelves and built-in furniture.

With cob you can create strong, structural walls of any size and height. It is (and has been) used all over the world, from palaces and 10 story buildings in the Middle East to 300 year old houses in England to small cottages in the southern and western United States. Cob is also used to make fireplaces, garden walls, benches, ovens, saunas, kids playhouses, and much more!

Mother and child
trimming a cob wall...

Light straw-clay

This is an infill technique for framed walls. Usually a wooden framework provides the skeleton structure. Straw is lightly coated with a clay-soil and water mixture (referred to as "Clay slip") and is tamped in between the wooden posts or studs. Boards are attached to the inside and outside of the wall to create a temporary form. The boards are removed as soon as each level of Light straw-clay is tamped into place and then re-attached for the next layer, which can be added right away. This technique creates very straight, insulated, solid walls.

Light straw-clay, sometimes called slip-straw, can be used for new conventional construction, taking the place of drywall, plastic, fiberglass insulation, plywood, and siding. Similarly, it can be used in remodels or to add an interior wall in an existing house. In many countries (in particular Germany and Japan), it has been used as an infill method for timber frame houses for centuries. It can also be used in a loose form rather than tamped, and stuffed into ceilings and wall cavities as a form of insulation. The clay-soil makes it more fire and rodent resistant; rodents don't like to get the fine clay particles in their teeth.

Straw-clay plaster

This is a mixture of the same clay slip used for light straw-clay, but mixed with chopped straw instead of long straw. Sometimes a little sand is added. As you add more and more straw to the slip, the material takes on a thick, chocolate mousse consistency, not liquid anymore but still quite wet. It can be mixed by hand in a shallow hole in the ground, with a shovel or hoe in a wheelbarrow, or on a tarp.

The high clay-soil content makes it very sticky, and the chopped straw provides both tensile strength and structure. It can be applied to a wall up to two inches thick. This makes it ideal for smoothing out irregular surfaces such as cob and straw bale walls in order to prepare them for a finish earthen plaster. This is often referred to as a brown coat. It can also be used as a "putty" to seal in windows (replacing foam and silicone sealants), to fix cracks and holes, to round hard edges, and to add three-dimensional art to surfaces. In combination with hardware cloth or chicken wire, you can create your own earthen drywall in any shape, horizontally or vertically, making it possible to build earthen ceilings and rounded, sculptural details around windows and doors. Or, you can apply this plaster to a woven mat of sticks and saplings, a technique called "wattle and daub" which has been used for millennia to create simple mud huts and thin partition walls.

Earthen Blocks

Using earthen material in a block form is a technique that has been widely used around the world, from the Great Wall of China to the missions on the California coast. To make blocks, a wet earthen mixture is poured or pressed into a wooden form. The form is removed and the block is allowed to dry in the sun. The earthen mixture used to make the block may be mostly clay-soil, mostly straw, or somewhere in between, depending on the materials that are available and the intended use of the block. The advantage of using blocks is that they can be made in advance, and then the structure can be built from the dried blocks in a relatively short amount of time. While raising a wall, blocks are stacked with a clay-soil mortar between them to seal cracks and hold the blocks together.

Tamped earthbags

For this technique, polypropylene plastic bags are filled with moist clay-soil, and then laid next to one another and tamped flat. When rivers flood, communities use these bags filled with sand to keep the water from overtaking their town. With a little more care and attention, these flood bags can become building blocks. Once the bags are protected from sunlight with a plaster or rock facade, they can last for hundreds of years. Earthbags can be a low-tech solution for stem walls (foundations) to protect earthen buildings from ground moisture. They are also used to build garden walls, terraces, or even whole houses. Tamping earth to create walls is not new. Rammed earth, a technique developed in France and practiced widely in Morocco, as well as rammed tires, popularized through the building of "earthships" in the southwest of the USA, are two other forms of using tamped earth. We have found earthbags to be the most practical and user friendly of the tamped earth techniques.

Earthen finish plasters

Earthen finish plasters are used to beautify and protect walls. They are a mixture of finely screened sand and clay-soil, sometimes amended with finely chopped straw or other available fibers. Enough water is added to turn the material into a cake batter consistency. It is then troweled on any prepared wall surface or system: cob, straw bale, plywood, concrete block, or drywall. Because it is usually applied no thicker than 1/4 inch, it is important that the surface it is applied to is relatively smooth. Earthen plasters can be made any color by choosing certain colors of clays and/or by adding pigments to the mix. Earthen plasters troweled smooth and hard create a water resistant protective layer for earthen walls.

Earthen floors

An earthen floor is a very smooth, hard, finished earthen layer on top of any solid subsurface, such as plywood, OSB ("oriented strand board," sometimes called chipboard), concrete, tamped gravel, or cob. The earthen floor mix contains a high percentage of sand with just enough clay to hold it together, as well as a good amount of finely chopped straw. Mixed to a thick cake batter consistency, the wet material is applied with a trowel, usually about ¾" thick. Once dry, an earthen floor is sealed with linseed oil, making it water resistant, dust free, and long lasting. Earthen floors are inexpensive, warm, beautiful, and comfortable to stand on. They also add a lot of thermal mass to a house, which helps to moderate daily temperature fluctuations.

Clay paints

Screened clay-soil or purchased powder clay can be mixed with water to make a clay slip which becomes the base for a clay paint. Usually, flour paste, pigments, and sometimes a little fine sand is added to provide a dust free, colorful, durable paint. Clay paints can be applied with a brush or a paint roller to an earthen plaster or directly onto plywood, concrete, or drywall. The color and texture of a clay paint is soft and pleasing. They are also very useful for creating interior and exterior murals.

Overview of Techniques

Technique name	Main Ingredients	Usage	Consistency
Cob	Sand Straw Clay-soil	Structural walls Blocks	Wet, like soft modeling clay
Light straw-clay	Straw Clay-soil	Infill, usually in stud or timber-frame walls Blocks	Dry straw, lightly coated with clay slip
Straw clay plaster	Straw Clay-soil Sometimes sand	Brown coat on any material 3D "Relief" plaster Ceilings Blocks	Chocolate mousse
Earthen blocks	Clay-soil Sand Straw	Structural walls	Dried blocks, mortared with soupy clay-soil
Earthbags	Clay-soil Sometimes straw	Foundations Structural walls	Moist clay-soil tamped in plastic bags
Earthen finish plasters	Sand Clay-soil Sometimes straw	Finish coat on wide variety of materials	Smooth cake batter
Earthen floors	Sand Clay-soil Straw	Finished, durable floors	A stiff cake batter
Clay paints	Clay Flour paste Sometimes sand	Paint on wide variety of surfaces	Paint-like

This may be helpful…
Regenerative building

There are phenomena in life where something gets created out of seemingly nothing. One can garden in a way that constantly makes the garden better, healthier, more productive, and more beautiful, mostly by understanding how nature works, how soil gets built, how water flows, etc. There is little or no cost involved, just steady work in a way that regenerates the land rather than degrades it.

A popular buzzword for today's builders is "sustainability." Builders and their clients want to create structures that are "sustainable," meaning they have little or no net impact on the environmental world. In theory, a truly sustainable building would produce as much energy as it used, and be built with materials that were "sustainably harvested" (meaning the rate and quantity of the harvest could be maintained indefinitely). The implication here is that our buildings, and our lifestyle, can have a "zero" net impact on the natural world.

This concept of sustainability, however, goes against the laws of nature. It implies that things can continue unchanged indefinitely, in a state of perfect stasis. But in nature, everything is always in flux, nothing stays the same for long. Our understanding of sustainability is further complicated by the fact that we live in a finite world, and our ability to use resources (i.e. building materials) must be considered against the rate at which others are also using these limited resources. For example, even though I live in a very modest 1,000 sq ft house, that uses a very small amount of wood and energy compared to my neighbor's 3,000 sq ft house, my house is still 2 or 3 times larger than the average house worldwide. If everyone on the planet were to build a 1,000 sq ft house, it would become instantly unsustainable! For those of us that truly care for life on earth, idealizing "sustainability" as our goal is limiting, unrealistic, and even deceptive.

A better word to use to describe our goals for building and living is the word "regenerative." Regenerative building and design means that we are working to actively enrich the life-giving systems of the world around us, by promoting healthy ecosystems. The result of this process is not simply leaving things in more or less the same state (i.e. sustainability), but actually making them better. If we want life on earth to be good, regenerative building and living is the only real chance we have for success.

Earthen materials are a great choice for regenerative building practices. Earthen walls are just re-formed earth, requiring no chemical changes or energy inputs. What used to be clay-soil in one spot becomes a beautiful shelter in another spot. This in and of itself does not create a "regenerative" building. However, as we harvest our clay-soil we have the unique ability to transform the land in ways that promote life. A hole dug in the right spot can become a pond, attracting wildlife and creating a greater bio-diversity. Or perhaps we would choose to dig swales, reducing run-off and encouraging new plant life.

Damaged areas are ideal sites for regenerative building practices. An abandoned mining site can be restored by moving earth around. Trash can be cleaned up and used to build with, either as fill in a wall, or as other useful features: an old tailgate can become a built-in shelf, broken glass can become drainage material below the foundation, bottles can bring in beautiful diffuse light into the house. Once the house is finished and people move in, they will start to clean up around the house, plant shrubs and trees, manage water and build soil. This idea goes against most people's instinct to build a house in a beautiful pristine location. But the reality is that as soon as you start building on a beautiful patch of land, you destroy what was attractive about it in the first place. Better to pick an already damaged piece of land, and then improve it!

Other building materials can also be harvested regeneratively. Wood for the roof can be harvested from locally grown trees, cut in a way that will stimulate the health of the forest. In the Western United States, years of clear-cutting and poor forestry practices have created millions of acres of forest that are overgrown with small diameter trees. Selectively thinning these forests will help the remaining trees to grow larger, which increases forest diversity and reduces the impact of wildfire. Using the harvested wood in its natural round form is also a "regenerative" choice, because it does not require the use of complicated machinery to mill it into dimensional lumber, and because we can use small diameter trees instead of having to cut large (and old) trees. Earthen materials work with round wood because the materials can be sculpted around the irregularly shaped poles.

Poor quality soils can be brought back to life by growing cover crops, like rye. Its roots help break up compacted earth, the seed heads can provide food for humans or animals, and dead stalks can be turned into compost or dried and used as fiber in your earthen building mix. The long rye stalks could even be used to make a thatched roof! Although not as long lasting as thatch made from traditional reeds and not so easy without some serious training, this could be a fun project to experiment with.

Last but not least, building with earth brings people together by promoting working in community to create healthy and beautiful houses. This process promotes positive emotions, strengthening human bonds and relationships. We could argue that this is the most important regenerative building we could do: that loving and caring for others is the ultimate life-enhancing act. Life can become pretty good if we start looking at it not as a balancing act or something to be simply "sustained," but rather as something to be improved and "regenerated."

1.3 Clay-soil

Visit www.HouseAlive.org *for pictures and videos on this chapter.*

All the discussed techniques use some combination of clay-soil, sand, and straw. Of these three ingredients, clay-soil is the most important one. It is the clay in the soil that makes building with earth possible as it holds everything together.

The following ingredients can often be found in soil:
· Sand (rocks broken up into small pieces)
· Silt (sand broken up into very small pieces)
· Organic matter (decomposed materials)
· Clay

If the soil is mostly organic matter, it is often referred to as topsoil and is great for growing food but impossible to build with. If it is mostly sand or silt, like on the beach or in the desert, it can be used as the sand in one of the building methods, but without adding clay-soil, it won't work.

Silt is essentially very tiny sand particles that have broken down to an almost powdery consistency. Silt is not useful as a building material although some silt in the clay-soil won't hurt. Because the silt particles are very fine and appear a little sticky when wet, silt is sometimes confused with clay. You will find, however, that a little ball of dried silt will easily fall apart if you squeeze it, which is something that does not happen with clay.

Clay particles are microscopically small (hundreds of times smaller than sand) and are shaped like plates. These platelets bond with water and form a sticky material that will be familiar to anyone who has ever played with clay. In the process of mixing with water, the dry clay swells and sticks to everything it comes in contact with. When it dries it shrinks and becomes hard again. Hence, pottery!

You can find soil that contains sufficient clay to build with nearly everywhere just by digging in the ground beneath your feet. Sometimes you will first find a few inches or more of topsoil before the color and consistency change and it turns into clay-soil. The soil consistency may vary dramatically from one place to the next due to natural and geological events such as past floods, landslides, volcanic action, and erosion patterns. The clay content in the soil can be dramatically different by moving a small distance in any direction. Suitable soil only needs to contain about 10% clay. Too much clay can actually make your work harder as it may become difficult to break up the soil, but the margins for useable clay-soil are very wide.

In hilly country clay-soil can often be seen in road cuts as a distinctive reddish color of soil often above solid rock. Pure clay and clay-soil is often this reddish color, but it can also be grey, black, or orange, and in rare cases blue, green, purple, and white. Clay-soil is also made visible by cracks in the surface soil, often seen on dirt roads or dried lakebeds. After a rain the soil dries and the clay shrinks, causing the surface to crack. Puddles and natural ponds can also be indicators of soil with high clay content. This is because clay particles bond to water and swell, making the soil water-resistant and slowing drainage.

You may at times find pockets of almost pure clay, formed over millions of years from rock, but never mixed with sand, silt, or organic matter. These places are also great for mining clay for pottery and other industries needing this more or less pure form. If you have difficulty locating clay-soil in your area, it can help to contact people who dig with big machines (backhoes). Farmers also often have good knowledge of local soils. These people know what clay is and often don't want it. They may even give you a load for free.

Testing clay-soil

To see if your soil has enough clay for building, you need to do tests and make samples.

Tests: Take a small amount of dry soil that you hope has some clay in it, about the size of a plum, make it wet, and start kneading it until it turns into a putty-like consistency. After a minute or so, you should look for four qualities:

- Stickiness: See how well it sticks to your hand: Flatten it in your palm and hold your hand open with your palm facing down. The clay should stick for at least a few moments before falling off.
- Sound: While kneading the wet mix, the sound changes and becomes "squishy," like the sound of someone chewing gum loudly.
- Shininess: The surface of the wet mix will take on a shiny appearance, caused by the water filling in the spaces between the clay particles.
- Moldability: The material should easily hold the shape of whatever you mold it into.

Once these four qualities have been confirmed, you know there is enough clay in your soil for building and you can go to the next step.

Samples: Make several test batches using the building technique you plan to use. You can add sand and straw in different proportions, let it dry, and check for these qualities of your samples:

- Workability: Is it easy to build with; does it stick well enough? This will tell you if there is enough clay and, in some cases, not too much straw in the mix.
- Strength/cohesion: Does it crack after it dries? This will tell you if there is too much clay in the mix or, in some cases, not enough straw. Does it crumble easily or dust? This is indicator of not enough clay.
- Suitability: Will it serve your purpose? This is different for each technique. For example, you want a cob wall to be strong and perhaps load-bearing, while you want an earthen plaster to be smooth and dust free.

Your tests should be representative of your project. For cob, build a small section of a wall at least one foot high, and for an earthen plaster put your test batch on the surface you will apply it to, covering about a square yard.

To make things more interesting, not only do different soils have different amounts of clay in them, but no two clays perform alike. They vary a bit in how much they swell and shrink and to what extent they become sticky. There are wide margins of what makes an acceptable clay-soil or mix. This is definitely more play than science. These variables, among other factors, set building with earth apart from most other building methods. Builders have the freedom and ability to compose their own unique combination of materials rather than using prescribed materials and recipes. A little knowledge and experience can set us free from the cost and damage caused by industrial building materials and provide us with a superior finished product.

The shake test

A shake test is another way to learn about your soil's contents. Fill a glass jar halfway with soil and the remaining half with water. Put the lid on and shake the jar really well for a minute. Let the contents settle for a few hours. The heaviest material, sand and gravel, will sink to the bottom right away, followed shortly after by silt. The clay will stay suspended in the water the longest and will slowly (most of it within a few hours) settle out over time. You can determine to what extend the clay has settled by how clear the water has become; cloudiness in the water is caused by clay. Organic matter will usually float on the surface.

Preparing clay-soil

More often than not, clay-soil will need some form of preparation before other materials can be mixed with it. The preparation can involve two different actions: hydrating and screening.

Hydrating: To what extend the clay-soil needs to be hydrated depends on a variety of factors. First, if the clay-soil is chunky, hard and dry, it is very hard to mix other materials with it. Therefore, hydrating it by soaking it in a bucket or tub will be helpful. If the clay-soil can easily be dug up with a shovel and is moist, gooey or powdery, hydrating may not be necessary at all. Second, consider the building technique you are planning on using the clay-soil for. For cob and earth bags, a moist clay-soil can work, so little or no hydration is needed. For light straw-clay, straw-clay plaster, earthen finish plasters, floors and paints a soupier mix in the form of clay slip is usually needed. This can be achieved by adding more water to a bucket of soaked clay-soil and then stirring it with your hands, a shovel, or a drill with a paint paddle attachment. When the clay is powdery or dissolves easily in water, simply putting it dry into a wheelbarrow and mixing in water with a hoe can do the trick. Whenever you hydrate dry clay, it usually works better to start with a little water in the bottom of the bucket, tub, or wheelbarrow, in order to avoid dry spots.

Screening: For cob, earth bags and blocks made out of cob, screening is usually not necessary. Sometimes, when we mix the material barefoot, its nice to screen sharp rocks out of the clay-soil. Aside from that, just pick out the bigger rocks with your hands. For light straw-clay and straw-clay plaster, it is nice to make sure that all the material can go through a ½" screen. Sometimes, your clay-soil may not have any rocks that size, so no screening would be necessary. For earthen floors, the material should go through a ¼" screen. For plasters and paints the material should go through a 1/16" screen (window screen). The most common type of screen used for all but the 1/16" screen is called "hardware cloth." It is made from galvanized steel and the intersections are welded together. It can be found at any hardware store.

Although you can easily mix cob with dry clay-soil, sometimes it can speed up the mixing process significantly just by hydrating the clay-soil in a bucket or tub, even just for 15 minutes. In some situations you may first screen and then hydrate, other times you may do it the other way around. A lot of that will have to do with the quality of your clay-soil. Through a little experimentation, you will quickly discover what works best for you.

Overview of Clay-soil

	Quality of clay soil
Cob	No chunks, large rocks picked out by hand, loose and powdery or soaked in buckets
Light straw-clay	Thin slip, 1/2 inch screened
Straw-clay plaster	Thick Slip, 1/2 inch screened
Block building	Depending on type of block, see above 3 methods
Earthbags	Moist soil, unscreened, rocks and chunks ok
Earthen plasters	Finely screened, powdery or soaked
Earthen floors	⅛" screened, powdery or soaked
Earthen paints	Slip, finely screened

This may be helpful…

What will it cost?

Many people consider building with earth because it has a reputation as a very inexpensive way to build. After all, you just dig up the dirt around your building site and turn it into walls. These houses can literally be "dirt cheap". Is this true? Not really. They can be very inexpensive, but this is usually not because of the inexpensive materials used for the walls.

Let's first look at the material cost of wall systems. Although digging up the dirt around your site might be cheap, most people still have to import straw and sand. Sometimes the ground is prohibitively hard and equipment is brought in to do some of the digging. If you then take into account that it may take you longer to build with earthen materials than to frame a wall with 2x4's you may discover that the cost of the materials for the wall ends up not being much cheaper than that of conventional buildings. This is partly so because conventional building materials (dimensional lumber, drywall, plywood) are mined, harvested, and mass-produced without much care for the earth and are therefore ridiculously cheap.

Typically, though, the quality of an earthen wall is much greater than that of a conventionally built wall. This creates what we could call secondary cost savings: The building needs less heating and cooling, doesn't make us sick, needs less maintenance, and we like it so much that we don't want to move. These cost savings, which are not directly related to the building process and stretch out over a longer period of time, already make it worthwhile to consider earthen construction.

There are of course cost savings to be found in the building process too. Here are some reasons why people can build an earthen house for a song.

Earthen materials are well suited for "Owner-builders," i.e. you can do most (or all) of the work yourself. This can make a house a lot less expensive, assuming you don't make huge mistakes because of inexperience (take a workshop!). Of course you have to take into consideration that while you are building you are often not able to work a job to make money. For many of us this requires careful financial planning.

Earthen buildings tend to be smaller. Smaller buildings require fewer materials and take less time to build, making them less expensive. Because of its beauty, sculptural qualities, built-in furniture and "roundish" character, you can often be as comfortable in a cob house half the size or less of what you feel you would need in a conventional house. Small spaces don't feel cramped because you actually like to be close to the walls.

Kitchens and bathrooms can be kept simple. Even a poor quality kitchen or bathroom in a conventional house can run you $10,000 and up. It's not unusual for them to start falling apart after the first year and be ready for the dump after 10 years. An earthen builder may be content with a wooden counter, a second-hand range and a sink, which can all be put together for under $250 and can provide a comfortable place to prepare food. Bathrooms can be reimagined to include homemade composting toilets, sponge baths and outdoor bathing places, eliminating the need for expensive plumbing.

Earthen walls make it possible to integrate found objects in a beautiful and practical way. The weirdest items can look good in the wall! An old piece of driftwood as a coat hook, a hubcap as a built-in shelf, odd shaped rocks as aesthetic features, you name it and it almost always looks good. Recycled and reused materials look great and are incredibly easy to integrate because of the stickiness of the clay and the fact that you can sculpt it in just about any shape.

Second-hand windows and doors can be creatively integrated into earthen walls. Quality windows and doors can be one of the single biggest-ticket items for a homebuilder. A nice custom-built window can easily cost over $1000! However it is possible to find windows at greatly reduced prices, even free, if you look for them. Check with contractors doing remodeling work, or window suppliers (sometimes people don't pick up their orders), or junkyards. It's a good idea to start collecting windows a year before you plan to start building. Once you have a nice selection, you can actually design your house to take into consideration the windows you have already collected.

In wealthier countries, earthen buildings are often not built to code. This frees the builder from building according to standards that were written in part because the building industry pushed for them or because of excessive liability fears. Some code regulations do make sense and have made buildings safer, but it has become very expensive to build to these standards. Of course, if you're building an unpermitted building you don't have to pay for permits either. This all adds up. I estimate that one could save up to 30% of the building cost by skipping the permitting process while still having the same house in terms of quality, size and safety.

Earthen buildings are mostly not seen as an "investment property". More likely, people choose to build with earth because they want to leave the world of housing speculation. They want to find a real home, a place to put down roots. Because cob buildings can be so inexpensive, there is also no need for loans and therefore no need for collateral and the requirements that come with that. Insurance policies can be skipped and property taxes will likely be lower.

Many earthen cottages were built (with permission) on other people's land. This eliminates the cost of the "building lot." And why not: "How can you own the land?" Chief Seattle rightfully asked us. Although these agreements feel like something that our capitalist culture does not approve of, it happens all the time: people with very little money and income end up sharing land and resources with the legal property owner, settling in a place that feels like their own. Especially in rural areas, this may work out well for the property owner; help is always welcome when managing a piece of land.

With a little creativity, a lot of hard work, and some rethinking of your ideas about property ownership, you can have a nice place to live for very little money. People with little building experience have built themselves and their families a beautiful little house for under $5000, and a lot of time and love.

1.4 Sand

Visit www.HouseAlive.org *for pictures and videos on this chapter.*

Sand is the least complex ingredient of the earthen construction methods. Sand is essentially broken down rocks, a result of centuries of erosion by wind, water, freezing, wave action, and floods. You can often find sand in areas where rocks erode: beaches, deserts, mountains, and riverbeds. You may also find that there is some sand already in your soil.

Sand provides the structure and strength in the mix. Think of sand as very small rocks. It is really the primary building block in load-bearing earthen building techniques such as cob and Adobe brick. Clay particles on their own are good at holding things together but not good at resisting compressive forces; thus the sand is needed to make a wall that can support a lot a weight without crumbling or collapsing. When sand is mixed with wet clay-soil, the clay particles surround and stick to each grain of sand. Once the clay dries and shrinks, the grains of sand get "locked" together. The more angular, rough, and sharp the sand is, the better this locking mechanism will be. To understand this, visualize building a tower out of marbles versus a tower out of blocks: the block tower will be more stable and can support more weight.

The sizes of the sand grains are also an important consideration. For structural wall systems such as cob, adobe block, and earthbags, it helps if the sand consists of grains that have different sizes, ranging from large to tiny. The smaller grains of sand can fill in the spaces between the larger ones, creating a very dense and tightly packed structure.

For finishes such as earthen plasters and clay paints, you don't need the range of different sizes. You still want the sand to be angular, but in order to get a smooth finish you want all the particles to be small. With earthen floors, there is some flexibility. The rougher the sand you use, the less polished the surface of the floor will be, but the floor will be stronger.

In straw-clay plaster the lack of sand is compensated for by an enormous amount of straw, still making for a structurally strong building material. Sand is occasionally added if the clay in the soil is so powerful that even the straw cannot prevent large cracks from forming when dry.

Locating sand

If you harvest sand yourself, you may encounter any size or shape, depending on where you find it and how eroded it is. Beach sand tends to be smaller and rounder, but not always. On the banks of rivers, the sand tends to get smaller and rounder the further it gets from the headwaters and the closer it gets to the ocean. In deserts, mountains, and plains, geological age and weather patterns can create a wide variety of qualities in sand.

If you cannot locate good sand nearby and there is not enough mixed in with your clay-soil, you can opt to buy sand. Fortunately for earthen builders, sand is widely available anywhere people are mixing concrete, as concrete needs sand for structure just like earthen materials do. Thus you can buy the right kind of sand for building structural walls almost anywhere. This "concrete sand," as it is often referred to, has varying grain sizes that are angular in shape. It is either harvested from the environment nearby or manufactured by crushing larger rocks. The final material is screened to ensure a consistent product. For larger projects like cob houses, people often buy concrete sand by the truckload and have it delivered. Generally speaking, the further you are from the people who sell it, the more expensive it becomes; a major part of the cost is the delivery.

For earthen plasters you can process sand yourself by screening purchased or harvested sand through a window screen. If you want more control over the color of your plaster, you are better off finding or buying light colored sand, sometimes sold under the name "Monterey Beach sand." You can then add pigments to get the desired color. When buying bags of sand, you can choose between different grain sizes. Grit sizes of #30 to #70 works well with earthen plasters (the larger the number, the smaller the grains); you can mix different grit sizes to achieve different results. For paints you may even select a finer grit. If color is not an issue and you would be happy with a somewhat rougher plaster, you can also choose to buy "plaster sand", usually used for stucco cement plasters, which is somewhat finer than concrete sand. This can make a lot of sense for exterior, somewhat rougher earth colored plasters.

How much sand?

It is important to determine how much sand to add to your clay-soil. You usually want to add enough sand so that once it is well mixed with clay-soil, the material is still sticky enough to build with. This can be different for cob than it would be for earthen plasters or floors. For example, if your plaster does not stick to the wall, it may have too much sand in it; an earthen floor won't have this problem because it doesn't have to fight gravity and therefore can have a much higher percentage of sand.

For cob and other similar materials, it is very common to use about 1 part clay-soil to 1 part sand. In some situations, if working with very pure clay, as much as 3 or 4 parts sand may be used for each part of clay-soil. We have also seen situations where the soil dug from the ground contains a good naturally occurring ratio of sand to clay, and no sand needs to be added at all. We call this "ready-mix."

Overview of Sand

	Sand?	Consistency
Cob	Yes	"Concrete sand" Varying fine to Coarse, angular
Light straw-clay	No	
Straw-clay plaster	Seldom	Any sand
Block building	Sometimes	Concrete sand
Earthbags	Optional	Any sand
Earthen plasters	Yes	Finely screened
Earthen floors	Yes	Coarse to fine, screened
Clay paints	Sometimes	Very finely screened

This may be helpful...

How to calculate the amount of materials you need

At some point in every project you will have to calculate how much material you will need to harvest or purchase. Below is a suggested method for doing so:

Calculate the volume of material you'll need in cubic feet. Volume is calculated by multiplying the length x width x thickness. It often helps to convert fractions into decimals, as you can then use a calculator. So, if a cob wall is 7 feet high, 20 feet long and 18 inches (1.5 foot) thick, the volume of the wall is:

7' x 20' x 1.5' = 210 cubic feet.

Plasters are often only 1/4 inch thick, or even thinner. Here too, you will have to convert inches into feet. ¼" is .021'. So, a ¼" plaster on a wall that is 6 feet high, 8 feet long would require about 1 cubic foot of material:

6' x 8' x .021' = 1 cubic feet.

Gather more materials than you calculate you'll need. You always lose a little and want to make sure you have plenty of extra. For cob I don't factor in the volume of the straw; once I have my cubic feet of the wall calculated, I then see how much sand and clay-soil I may need. For example, if the walls of my house are 3000 cubic feet, and I have determined that my cob mix will need to be 1 part sand to 2 parts clay-soil, I will need 1000 cubic feet of sand and 2000 cubic feet of clay-soil. For a greater margin of safety, don't subtract the area of the windows or doors, especially if they only take up a small part of the wall.

If you order materials by the truckload from a gravel yard, you will have to convert from cubic feet to cubic yards. A cubic yard measures 3'x3'x3' and therefore equals 27 cubic feet.

There are almost 7.5 gallons (7.48 to be precise) in one cubic foot. This is handy to know when you are working with buckets. A standard bucket holds about 5 gallons, but you usually don't fill it up with more than 3 or 4 gallons of material. That means that a cob batch made with about 2 buckets of raw material (3 to 4 gallons per bucket) will result in about 1 cubic foot of mixed cob. This will help you to calculate how many batches are needed to build the walls of your house, so you can set daily goals and calculate progress!

We've found that when using finely sifted clay, the small clay particles fill the spaces between the sand grains and therefore don't contribute as much to the overall volume of the mix. This is especially true for plasters and floors. In this situation, it's recommended that you increase the volume of materials you harvest (or purchase) by 20-30%.

It's difficult to calculate the volume of straw you'll need. A tightly compacted bale will have a lot more straw than a loose bale. Straw is inexpensive so make sure to get enough. Extra bales make nice seats and scaffolding and leftover loose straw can be used in your garden.

Here are few useful conversions to know. The smaller measurements can be useful when adding pigments to plasters or when making small test batches.

1 cubic yard = 27 cubic feet	1 cubic foot = 7.5 gallons
1 gallon = 4 quarts	1 quart = 4 cups
1 cup = 16 tablespoons	1 tablespoon = 3 teaspoons

...and for the metrically minded people: A cubic meter is 1000 liter and a bucket holds about 20 liters.

1.5 Straw

Visit www.HouseAlive.org for pictures and videos on this chapter.

Straw has many different functions in earthen building, the most common being strength. Strands of straw give earthen materials enormous tensile strength, making it hard for them to be pulled apart. Individual strands are relatively weak and can be broken by hand, but many strands combined in close proximity are extremely strong. In addition to strength, straw can also provide insulation value, warmth, softness, and beauty to earthen building materials.

What is straw?

Straw is a product of grain farming and is the leftover stalks after the grain heads have been harvested. It has high silica content with little nutritional value for animals. It decomposes slowly and can last centuries if kept dry, dark, and surrounded by clay-soil. It is often confused with hay; however, "hay is for horses," and is made from dried grasses to provide feed for animals with no access to pasture. Any kind of straw will work for earthen construction: wheat, barley, oat, rye, rice, and more. Straw tends to be stronger if it is from a recent crop and stored in a dry, dark place.

Before straw is baled, the stalks are usually chopped up in the field by a machine called a "combine." Different types of combines chop straw into different lengths. Almost all straw works for all the earthen building techniques, but if you have a choice, you may want to pick a length that is appropriate for what you are planning to do. Avoid straw that is moldy. Moldy straw turns different colors like black or light grey. If you have nothing else around, you can let it dry in the sun, effectively killing the mold. Otherwise, get a different bale and use the moldy straw in the compost pile.

The most common ways that straw is baled are with two strings or with three strings. Two-string bales tend to have longer straw because they were usually cut by older, less powerful combines. They are easier to lift and handle, and many builders prefer them. In the United States a bale costs somewhere between $4 and $8. A small 200 square foot cob or adobe cabin may use between five and ten bales, depending on the techniques being used.

Straw is very easy to find and is relatively inexpensive. Where straw is not available or is too expensive, however, other options are often available. Many people have built without straw, using fibers from other plants, such as dried grasses or weeds, shredded paper, coconut husks, cornhusks, and more.

You can also grow your own grain, harvest the seeds, and use the straw for building. This will take some labor, as well as a good size plot of land. You will need about 1,000 square feet to grow one bale of straw. Many grains are easy and fun to grow and harvest. Sometimes we find grain growing on the outside walls of a new earthen building because some seed heads were not removed during the harvest process and ended up in the straw. The seeds then fell out in the building process and germinated, charming the building's first year with bunches of grain.

Straw in earthen building techniques

Cob
Straw makes cob incredibly strong. Thick cob walls with lots of long strands of straw in them are very hard to demolish, even with sledgehammers and power tools. The more straw you mix in with the cob, the stronger the wall will be. Although little serious testing has been done, one can imagine that a lot of straw can help a cob wall survive during an earthquake. Straw also gives a cob wall some insulation. It makes the material less dense, and it is therefore more difficult for heat to travel through the wall by means of conduction. In the building process, straw is what makes it possible to stack the material as a wet mix without the wall slumping like pudding. It also enables the builder to create shapes like niches, arches, and cantilevered shelves easily.

Light straw-clay
Straw is the main ingredient in light straw-clay, making up 90% or more of the volume. In light straw-clay the straw doesn't hold anything together like it does in cob, rather the straw becomes the wall itself, with the clay holding it together. This makes the wall very soft and insulative. A 10" thick finished wall has an insulation value of about R-15. But this material has many advantages over conventional insulation materials:

- The lack of hollow spaces in the wall prevents it from being a nesting ground for insects and rodents
- There is no sagging of insulation material over time, eliminating the emergence of "cold spots" in the wall
- It is inexpensive and non-toxic
- Finished with an earthen plaster, it easily lets water vapor travel through the wall, reducing the risk of mold
- The clay in the material adds mass to the wall, which makes for less drastic temperature swings
- Provides excellent sound insulation

Straw-clay plaster
For this technique, the straw is chopped into pieces of one to four inches and added to clay slip. The straw makes it stiff and interconnected so that it can be applied very

thick, even up to two inches. When dry, it becomes very strong and provides added insulation and mass to any wall or ceiling.

Earthen blocks
Straw can add a lot of strength to earthen blocks, which is helpful if you either don't have a lot of clay in your soil or you have too much clay in your soil, causing your blocks to crack when they dry. Adding more straw to a block creates more tensile strength and improves the insulative capacity of the block, but decreases the compressive strength making the block less load bearing.

Earthbags
Putting straw into an earthbag mix wouldn't make a lot of sense, nor would it create a problem. Normally straw is left out.

Earthen plasters
Straw is optional in earthen plasters. They work just fine without straw. Choosing to add straw will give a plaster more strength and warmth, in addition to creating a visual effect that can be pleasing. Straw added to plasters is usually finely chopped, to a length of about one inch or less. You can save yourself the work of chopping by adding dry horse manure sifted through a ¼" screen to your plaster. Manure contains many already chopped (chewed) fibers!

Earthen floors
Finely chopped straw, cut and/or screened to a length of one inch or smaller, is always added to earthen floors, making them warmer, softer, stronger, and more beautiful.

Paints
Speckles of straw can be added to clay paints purely for a visual effect.

Processing straw

For different earthen building techniques you need different lengths of straw. The straw can be:

- As is, the way it comes out of the bale, about 4 to 10 inches long
- Chopped, about 1 to 4 inches long
- Finely chopped, about an inch long or less.

The simplest way to chop straw without using a power tool is to bundle the straw and then chop it with a sharp machete on a wooden block. For all but the smallest projects, though, mechanized chopping often makes the most sense. Your best options usually involve a string turning at high RPM's. This could be a weed whacker held in a trashcan (make a hole in the lid to accommodate the handle.) You could also drive a string mower through a small pile of straw or use a leaf mulcher, putting the straw in from the top where it lands on a fast turning string. The latter has been found to be the most practical. A small electric or gas wood chipper/shredder can also be used.

For finer applications like floors and plasters, you may have to send the chopped material through the machine a second time and/or screen it to separate out the longer pieces. A ¼" screen stapled to a wooden frame will usually work fine for this purpose.

Older bales are more easily chopped as the straw is typically more brittle. Occasionally, you may find bales that were initially chopped up so aggressively by the combine that the straw is already relatively short to begin with. This straw is usually also easier to chop up further or screen to smaller lengths. In lieu of chopping, you can also ask the person selling you the straw if you can sweep his/her barn; you will usually end up with a pile of smaller pieces of straw that fell out of the bales.

Overview of Straw

	Function	Length
Cob	Tensile strength, insulation, workability	Long
Light straw-clay	Wall infill, insulation, plastering surface	Long
Straw-clay plaster	Tensile strength	Chopped
Block building	Tensile strength, insulation	Long
Earthbags	Seldom used	
Earthen plasters	Beauty, tensile strength, warmth	Finely chopped/screened
Earthen floors	Tensile strength, insulation, softness, beauty	Finely chopped/screened
Earthen paints	Beauty	Shredded or finely screened

1.6 Other Materials

All earthen building techniques use clay-soil, usually mixed with sand and/or straw. These three materials allow you to build almost anything. For some techniques additional ingredients are used.

Boiled linseed oil

Linseed oil is used in earthen floors, plasters, and paints to make the end product more durable. After earthen floors are dry, three or four coats of oil are applied. You have no choice but doing so in order for the floor to last. The oil makes the floor feel somewhat leathery, prevents dusting, and seals it so you can mop the floor. For plasters, 1 to 4 tablespoons of oil can be added to five gallons of mix, increasing the water resistance of the plaster. More can be added to clay paints to make the product resemble an oil paint.

Linseed oil can be purchased at hardware and paint stores and costs about $25 per gallon. Organic oils can be purchased online for around double the cost. It is important that you buy boiled linseed oil, rather than raw. The boiled oil will set and dry within a few days, while the raw type can take many days or even weeks to dry. Count on using between one and two gallons of oil per 100 square feet of floor space. See the "oiling earthen floors" section for more information.

Flour paste

Flour paste is made out of water and white flour and functions as glue in plasters and paints. The gluten in the flour prevents dusting and makes the plasters and paints smooth, silky, and pleasant to work with. Because you add stickiness without adding more clay, your plaster or paint will be less likely to crack. Flour paste can also be painted directly on an earthen plaster to stabilize it if it turned out dusty. It will provide an invisible layer of glue over the plaster.

When you add fine sand to flour paste, you can use a paint roller or brush to apply it to a smooth surface to prepare it for an earthen plaster. This is often done on concrete walls, plywood and painted or unpainted drywall. It dries quickly and gives the surface a sandpaper-like texture, making it easier for a earthen finish plaster to adhere to the wall.

Flour paste is easy to make. The trick is to activate the gluten in the white flour. Here's how it's done:
- Add one quart (4 cups) of white flour to two quarts of cold water and mix it to a paste-like consistency.

- Add this to six quarts of boiling water and mix it with a large whisk. Turn the stove to low.
- Keep stirring, ensuring that the bottom doesn't burn, until it has the consistency of thick gravy.
- Let it cool before use.

Don't add white flour directly to hot water or it will form chunks, making it impossible to create a smooth paste.

Flour paste will eventually go rancid. You can usually keep it for a few days in a cool place or a refrigerator. It is best to make in the evening what you estimate you will need the following day.

Iron oxides

Both potters and people working with concrete use iron oxides to color their work. For our purposes they can also work in earthen plasters, floors, and clay paints. Iron oxide is manufactured by oxidizing (rusting) iron under controlled conditions to create a range of colorful "earth-toned" pigments. Other types of oxides, such as copper and titanium, are also available in brighter colors like green and white; often these types of pigment are more toxic and dangerous to work with, so use caution and read the packaging carefully. You can also buy synthetic iron oxides that work just as well. Masonry and pottery supply stores are your best sources for pigments.

It is best to get pigment in a powder form and mix it with a little water before you add it to your plaster. The colors tend to be soft and natural, ranging from a pale yellow (ochre) to red, dark red (buff), and dark brown. When testing colors it is important to let the test dry before you evaluate the results, as the color shifts during the drying process.

Bagged clay

For earthen plasters and clay paints, people often buy clay in powdered form from pottery supply stores. This can be very useful if you want a light color but only have access to darker natural occurring clay-soils. Kaolin clay is very popular for this purpose because it adheres well, has a neutral, almost white color, and doesn't shrink very much when it dries. Of course there are other options and colors as well. The powdered clay often comes in 25 lbs paper bags and costs around $40 per bag. Because plasters and paints are relatively thin, you won't need very much; depending on the recipe you have developed, a bag of clay will be enough to plaster a decent sized room.

Manure

Both cow and horse manure can be welcome additives to earthen plasters and floors. One can have as much as 10% of the plaster consist of manure. Cow manure is useful for its enzymes, which make the plaster adhere better and increase durability. For this purpose, it is best to use fresh manure. Horse manure is used for the many fibers it contains, made of short pieces of undigested grasses and hay. It can add structure and beauty to any plaster. Let the horse manure dry out, so you can grate it over a ¼" screen to free up the fine pieces of fiber.

Borax
Borax is a naturally occurring mineral that is commonly available as a laundry additive and household cleaner. It is sometimes used as a mold inhibitor in plasters and floors. This is useful if you think it will take a long time for the plaster or floor to dry. One half cup per five gallons of material is about the right ratio to use. Dissolve the borax in a little warm water before adding it to your material. It can be purchased at the grocery store, sold in the aisle with the laundry detergents.

Burlap, chicken wire, and hardware cloth
All three of these materials are used to support straw-clay plaster or other plaster-like materials when making sculptural shapes around windows or to round corners. Another useful application of these materials is to avoid cracks in finish plasters where two different materials meet. A common example of this is where an earthen material meets a wooden post. Because the wood may move slightly, or shrink and contract due to variations in temperature and humidity levels, a finish earthen plaster will likely crack at the intersection. Bridging this intersection with any of the above materials can help prevent this from happening.

Earthbags
These are polypropylene bags that are filled with clay-soil to make foundations or walls. The smaller bags, about a foot wide and 2 feet long, can be found at hardware stores and are sold as "flood bags." The larger ones, about 1.5' x 3', are used for animal feed. You can often buy them where there is a grain elevator or get them for free from people who buy animal feed in these bags. You can also buy them online where you may have a greater choice of sizes. The width of the bag determines the width of your foundation or wall. Some people buy long tubes made out of the same material, fill up the whole tube with moist clay-soil, and seal the ends. This creates a wall with fewer seams.

Portland cement
Portland cement is a powder that when mixed with water undergoes an irreversible chemical reaction and dries hard. If you mix it with sand and gravel, you get concrete (1 part cement, 2 parts sand and 3 parts gravel). Generally speaking, cement and cement products should be avoided in buildings for humans. Cement sometimes contains toxic additives, concrete floors are hard and loud, and concrete walls and roofs overheat buildings in the summer and become very cold in the winter. In addition to these disadvantages, it also takes an incredible amount of energy to produce and transport cement and concrete, making its use one of the major contributors of greenhouse gases.

However, there are a few places in the earthen building process where a little cement can provide extra security, mainly when using earthbags for a foundation. By mixing about one shovel worth of cement for each full bucket of the moist clay-soil, the earthbag fill becomes stabilized. In other words, if the bags were to get soaking wet, or fail altogether (or both), the foundation could survive because the clay-soil would not become soft and deteriorate. Making sure there is some sand and/ or gravel in the mix will also help make it stronger. It won't be as strong as concrete because there is only a little cement in the mix, but experience has shown that it is strong enough to support an earthen house.

Other Materials

Cob	Nothing added
Light straw-clay	Nothing added
Straw-clay plaster	Burlap, chicken wire, or hardware cloth
Block building	Nothing added
Earthbags	Cement for the foundation
Earthen plasters	Pigments, flour paste, Borax
Earthen floors	Linseed oil, pigments, Borax
Earthen paints	Pigments, flour paste, Borax

1.7 Tools for earthen construction

Visit www.HouseAlive.org for pictures and videos on this chapter.

You won't need many tools when building with earth. The ingredients are minimally processed, easy to transport, and often applied by hand. Only basic hand tools are needed to do this work.

It is possible to continue adding more powerful tools to the building site. An earthen building site can be as loud, fast, dangerous, and unpleasant as any conventional building site. However, your experience of building will change, and so will the spirit of the house you are working on.

Buckets
Buckets are used for all earthen building techniques. The three main purposes for buckets are
• Soaking clay-soil
• Transporting materials
• Mixing clay slip, plasters, and paints.

They are also used to store materials and tools. The most common bucket holds five gallons. You can often locate free buckets at fast food restaurants or grocery stores. You can also buy buckets at home improvement stores. Make sure they have a solid handle otherwise they are impractical to carry, and avoid the soft-plastic ones as they break easily.

It is easier to carry two half-full buckets (one in each hand) than one full one. Doing so will save you a lot of energy and help avoid back injuries. To further protect your body, you can also acquire 2.5 - 3 gallon buckets, in effect forcing yourself not to carry too much. This makes it easier to include children and less strong adults in the work.

Buckets don't make good scaffolding. They are dangerous to stand on and will break easily under a person's weight. The sun is hard on buckets; uv light breaks down the plastic and makes it weaker. During work breaks, put the buckets in the shade or cover them with a tarp. There almost never seem to be enough buckets on a building site. Unless you are doing a small project by yourself, get as many buckets as you possibly can.

Wheelbarrows
Wheelbarrows are used to:
• Transport raw ingredients and materials that are ready to be used, such as cob, plasters or earthen floor mix
• Screen materials (Place the screen on top of the wheelbarrow)

- Mix materials, in particular light straw-clay, straw-clay plaster, earthen floor mix, and earthbag fill

Flat tires are always frustrating on the building site and can be avoided by investing in a solid tire, which is more expensive but longer lasting.

Hand truck (Dolly)
A hand truck or dolly is extremely useful for moving heavy buckets and tarp-loads of cob or other earthen materials. The advantage of using a dolly is that you do not need to lift the material up off the ground; the tool will do the lifting work for you, with the help of leverage.

Shovels

Shovels are used for digging up clay-soil and sand as well as for mixing clay-soil in a bucket or wheelbarrow. Any standard spade shovel will do.

Hoe

A hoe is used to mix materials in a wheelbarrow for plasters, earthen floors, or earthbags. It's easiest to do this with two people, one on either side of the wheelbarrow, switching sides from time to time to ensure that the material gets evenly mixed.

Tarps

Woven polypropylene tarps are extremely handy and used in many aspects of earthen building:
- A 6' x 8' tarp allows two people to mix cob quickly and efficiently
- Tarps are used to cover things so they don't dry out too fast in hot weather
- They can provide shade for people working as well as for plasters drying. Slowing the drying process can help prevent cracking
- During plastering and painting, they protect the floor from getting too muddy
- During rain, tarps can cover earthen projects in progress and keep tools and materials dry

Polypropylene tarps are usually blue, but also come in green and brown. They get serious use on the building site so plan on them wearing out quickly. Generally speaking, the cheaper the tarp you buy, the faster it wears. However, any free material that resembles the common blue tarp will work as well. One example is lumber wrap, which can usually be found in the dumpster of any large lumber store or home improvement center. Old billboards, broken tents, and tyvek sheets can also function as tarps.

Dull handsaws

A collection of dull handsaws will help you shape and trim cob walls. They can be made more effective by cutting larger teeth (about 1/2 inch) in them with an angle grinder. If a saw is long and can flex a little, it helps with trimming and shaping curved walls or rounded shapes. Also, cutting off the knob on the handle will make it easier to trim in different positions. The best places to find these dull saws are second hand stores and garage sales. Keep in mind that once you use a saw for cob, it will never again be useful for cutting wood!

Machete

A machete can also be used for trimming and shaping cob, as well as for chopping straw. It will dull quickly with that kind of use and will need to be sharpened regularly.

Leaf mulcher

Chopped straw can be produced through a combination of chopping it with a machete and screening, but a leaf mulcher can be really handy to produce large amounts of chopped straw. A commonly used variety looks like a plastic barrel with a weed whacker string turning inside. Loose straw is thrown in the top and a trash bag or can catches the chopped straw as it falls out the bottom of the machine. Sometimes it may be necessary to put the material through a second time. Even then, some additional screening is usually needed for earthen floors and earthen finish plasters. These machines are loud and create a lot of dust so make sure you wear a dust mask and ear protection.

Level

A level is used to ensure that your walls go up plumb, which means perpendicular to the earth. For most walls, a four-foot level works well. You can also tape a one-foot level against a very straight piece of wood four to eight feet long and it can work just the same. Some people hang a heavy object at the bottom of a string and use that as a guideline for the wall, referred to as a "plumb bob". This is especially handy for taller buildings built with blocks.

Levels are also used to ensure that horizontal surfaces are built level, which means parallel to the earth. Examples would be windowsills, shelves, and floors. Again, to measure distances longer than your level is long, tape a short level on a longer straight board. An easy way to find out if a board is straight is to hold it against another board of similar length. If they fit tightly together, both boards are most likely pretty straight. For very long distances, a line level can be used. This is a tiny level hung from a string. For the most accurate reading, make sure that the string is tight and that the level is hanging in the middle.

Drill and paint paddle

An electric drill with a paint paddle is very handy for mixing clay slip, earthen plasters, and clay paints in buckets. The paint paddle attachment is essentially a giant whisk that can be attached to the drill chuck. Corded drills tends to be easier to use as you don't have to change batteries all the time, and they also generally have stronger motors. A side handle on the drill will put less strain on your wrists. Keep electric tools clean and as mud-free as possible.

Flat tampers

These are usually 8" x 8" metal plates with a four foot wooden or fiberglass handle coming out of the middle. They are great for breaking up hard clay-soil, for compacting earthbags and for tamping a compacted-gravel subfloor (described in the "floor" chapter) in preparation for an earthen floor.

Screens

The most useful screen sizes are one-half inch, one-quarter inch, and window screen. The size used is determined by what the screened material is needed for. All but the window screen is made from hardware cloth (welded galvanized wire, square holes). For window screens, it is best to use the metal screen, as the fiberglass kinds break easily. All screens should be attached to a wooden frame with staples, tape, or nails. For larger screens, it is often helpful to attach a set of legs so it can stand at an angle.

Block forms
These are used to be filled with material in order to make earthen blocks. They are usually rectangular in shape and made out of sturdy wood. Corners can be reinforced with metal brackets or plywood screwed on top of the form. This will help the forms maintain their square corners.

Plastering tools
For finish plastering, applying a brown coat, and troweling earthen floors, we use plastering tools. For large, flat surfaces, pool trowels work best. These are trowels that are rounded on both sides and are flexible. Smaller ones, about eight inches long, are harder to find but easier to work with. Check with your local masonry supply store. Pool trowels are the tool of choice for earthen floors. For finer plasterwork, we recommend delicate Japanese trowels that are pointed on one end and made from very flexible stainless steel. The pointed shape makes them handy for getting into corners. They are a bit pricy but are a pleasure to work with and well worth the money, especially when working on relatively flat surfaces. You may not find them in local stores, but they can be purchased online.

The lids of plastic yogurt (or similar) containers are useful for plastering all types of surfaces and are available for free. Cut off the rim and you have a small, flexible, smooth disk. This tool especially shines when plastering rounded surfaces and three-dimensional features. Sometimes it is helpful to cut the lids in a particular shape to accommodate unique plaster details. Make sure to smooth jagged edges or irregularities on the plastic disk that could scratch the plaster.

Sponges, spray bottles, and misters
These tools are used to slightly moisten surfaces before a layer of fresh material is applied. Sponges are also used to smooth out trowel marks and imperfections from freshly plastered walls before they are completely dry.

Brushes and rollers
These tools are useful for all painting jobs and are used the same way as they would be for conventional painting. The roller can also be used to apply a base-coat of flour paste or clay slip to a conventional building material such as drywall or plywood.

Scaffolding and ladders

Working at the right height is essential for the well being of your body, and to ensure high quality work. For walls less than eight feet, straw bales make great scaffolding and can be stacked on top of each other if necessary. If you are working with a lot of people, a few planks between bales can increase the scaffolding space. Very handy, but a bit pricy, are folding aluminum steps, about 3 feet long and 20 inches high. They are very stable and easy to move around.

Once the wall is over eight feet, you need to use ladders or scaffolding. With very tall earthen walls, you can also build the scaffolding into the wall, simply by using wooden supports coming out of the wall. Once the building is done, you can then cut off these supports and plaster over the part that is still in the wall.

Safety tools

Gloves are useful for working with any clay-based materials. They protect your hands from getting small cuts as well as from drying out due to contact with the clay. They do, however, make you a little less coordinated with your hands and also make it harder to feel the subtle textures of the materials. Most people prefer the woven gloves with rubberized palms, often used by gardeners.

When screening, pouring, or measuring dry clay-soil or pure clay, there is often a cloud of clay-dust around you. It is best to stand upwind from your materials so the wind blows the dust away from you. If this is not possible, use a dust mask or a bandana around your mouth and nose. Inhaling any kind of very fine particles can be irritating to your lungs.

Overview of Tools

Cob	Buckets, shovel, wheelbarrow, tarp, dull hand saw, machete, level, screens
Light straw-clay	Buckets, hoe, wheelbarrow, screens
Straw-clay plaster	Buckets, hoe, wheelbarrow, screens, straw chopper, drill and paddle
Block building	All tools used to mix the earthen materials, block form, level
Earthbags	Shovel, hoe, wheelbarrow, tamper, level
Earthen plasters	Buckets, drill and paddle, screens, plastering tools
Earthen floors	Buckets, shovel, hoe, wheelbarrow, pool trowel, screens
Earthen paints	Buckets, drill and paddle, screens, brushes and rollers

This may be helpful…

Rhythm, routine and ritual

The joy you find in building, the quality of your work and the progress you make depends on a variety of factors, such as your skill level, your strength, the quality of your tools, your personality, even the weather. Probably least considered but nevertheless very valuable are a set of habits that can form the basis for a very satisfying relationship to your work and your project. If these habits are well integrated into your building practices, they can to a certain level compensate for a lower level of strength or skills, bad weather or a grumpy personality. These habits conveniently all start with the letter "R" and can become the foundation of your work patterns.

Rhythm

When working in a rhythm, things seem to take less effort. When rhythms get broken, people suddenly feel tired. Being a waiter in a restaurant is more tiring when it is not busy because it's hard to get into the work rhythm. On the building site it is often easier to first mix a whole bunch of material, say for an hour or so, stockpile it, and then build for an hour. Try that, rather than mixing a little and building a little. The mixing goes more smoothly and efficiently as time goes on, because you get into the rhythm of it. Another way to bring rhythm into your building work is through music. Singing, or a steady beat, either played live by a musician or from a recording, will make the act of building more like a dance.

Routine

A routine can help you to fully embrace the building process as part of your life in the presence, helping you to enjoy it, rather than focussing on just "getting it done". It can include starting and stopping at a certain time, having a long lunch break, cleaning up your tools at the end of the day, sharpening your tools every Friday, taking a water break after 5 batches of cob mixing, stretching every morning before you start, etc. These routines can become the framework for your day or week.

Rituals

Rituals can be brought into your building practice to help connect you to the context you work and live in. Taking time to express gratitude, hold a celebration, have conversations, offer prayers or practice meditation can all be forms of ritual. The expression of the ritual can be serious or light, depending on you and the people you work with: dance and music, facilitated sharing, or even cracking open a beer at the end of the day, are all various forms of ritual. Finding ones that feel good to you can bring meaning to what you are doing and help you form a story around your project.

Although it is good to consciously bring these habits into your building practices, be sure to change them up if they don't serve you. They should not become disciplines for discipline's sake! Rather, ask yourself: "What rhythms, routines and rituals can I bring into my building habits that will make my life and work more enjoyable?"

1.8 Wall Systems

Earthen building techniques can be combined with each other as well as with conventional building methods. It is the stickiness of the clay that makes all of these combinations possible. Any two materials containing clay can be used in combination. To ensure success, it helps if the receiving surface is dampened to activate the clay particles of that particular layer. This can be done with a sponge, spray bottle, or mister. When earthen materials are applied on smooth, conventional materials such as concrete or plywood, it helps to first apply a thin layer of clay slip painted on with a brush or paint roller. The different combinations of materials that can be used to create wall systems are really endless, but below are some of the more common ones.

Cob walls

Cob walls tend to be rough with lots of pieces of straw sticking out of the wall. It would not make sense to put a finish plaster on it right away. First, make it smoother with what is often called a brown coat. This can be a basic earthen plaster made from just sand and clay, or it can be a straw-clay plaster. The smoother you make this brown coat, the easier it will be to put a finish earthen plaster on it and the better your results will be. An optional clay paint can be used as a last decorative layer. However, a nicely plastered wall can lose some depth and character once you paint it.

It is not uncommon to finish the outside of a cob building with just a smooth brown coat. This makes the building fit in better with its surroundings, especially if the color of the clay matches that of the earth surrounding the building.

The wall from inside to outside:
Clay paint (optional)
Earthen finish plaster
Straw-clay or sand-clay plaster
COB
Straw-clay or sand-clay plaster
Earthen finish plaster (optional)

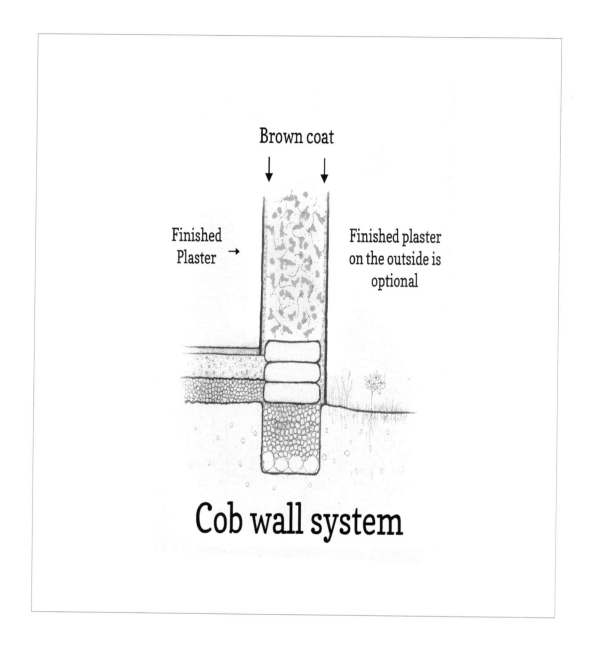

Cob wall system

Light straw-clay

Light straw-clay walls can be finished similarly to cob walls, except that the brown coat is always a straw-clay plaster: this can add needed strength to the wall and sticks better to the light straw-clay than just a simple clay-sand plaster. In addition, because of the high straw content, a straw-clay plaster will add some extra insulation to the wall system.

The wall from inside to outside:
Clay paint (optional)
Earthen finish plaster
Straw-clay plaster
LIGHT STRAW-CLAY
Thick clay slip (as a finish)
Straw-clay plaster
Earthen finish plaster (optional)

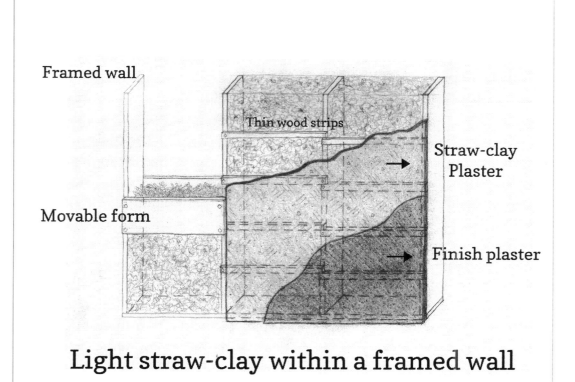

Light straw-clay within a framed wall

Earthbags

Earthbags can be a bit more challenging to transform into smooth walls because of the deep grooves and seams in between the layers of bags and because the polypropylene material is very slick, making it harder for clay based materials to stick to it. For these reasons it is best to first paint a layer of clay slip on the bags, followed by a straw-clay plaster that will fill in the seams and cover the outside of the bags. The seams can be an advantage here because of their somewhat horizontal surface; they provide a ledge for the plaster to sit on and adhere to. You then follow the same procedures as with cob or light straw-clay wall systems.

The wall from inside to outside:
Clay paint (optional)
Earthen finish plaster
Straw-clay plaster
Clay slip
EARTHBAGS
Clay slip
Straw-clay plaster
Earthen finish plaster (optional)

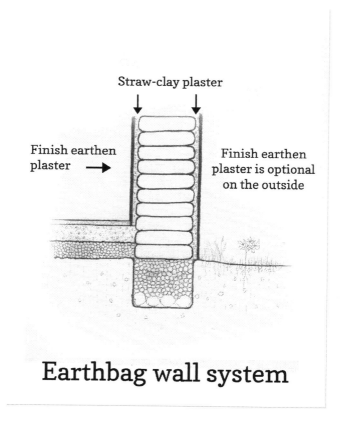

Earthbag wall system

Drywall with earthen materials

There is a lot of drywall in the world, and the use of earthen building techniques can give it some redeeming value. Clay paints can go directly on drywall, as can earthen plasters. If the drywall is painted or is a horizontal surface (like a ceiling), it sometimes helps to first apply a layer of flour paste with some sand mixed into it before you apply the earthen plaster. This gives the wall some roughness and makes it easier for the plaster to adhere.

You can also create "faux earthen walls," by first starting with a layer of straw-clay plaster before applying a finish earthen plaster. This will make the drywall appear more natural and organic because it won't be perfectly flat anymore. The straw-clay plaster can also be used to soften hard edges and to round corners, creating a less industrial and less manufactured look.

Wall possibilities from inside to outside:
Clay-paint
Earthen finish plaster
Straw-clay plaster
Flour paste/sand
Drywall
Conventional wall system can continue on towards the outside of the building.

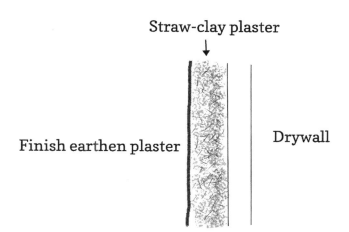

Straw-clay plaster

Finish earthen plaster

Drywall

From drywall to earthen wall

Other conventional materials

Other conventional materials can be combined with earthen materials in the same way as you would do it with drywall. On bare plywood it is best to first apply a layer of clay slip, which can actually penetrate the plywood a bit and make for a good connection with the next layer.

When working with concrete surfaces, make sure that there are no moisture issues with the concrete before you apply any earthen materials. Concrete is notorious for wicking moisture through capillary action, especially if it is in contact with the earth. A concrete floor or wall can actually weep moisture, making earthen materials vulnerable. Treating the concrete with a sealer first may be required.

Bridging materials

When two different types of materials meet, such as wood and cob, earthen finish plasters often crack along the intersection. This can be caused by movement in the actual building or because each material reacts differently to changes in humidity and temperature, expanding and contracting at different rates. To mitigate this you can bridge the two materials with a piece of burlap or hardware cloth. Make sure that there is at least an inch of overlap, but more is better. Staple or nail the cloth to both materials with at least one nail or staple per square inch. A hammer stapler is really handy for stapling on wood, nails or screws can be driven into cob or straw-clay plaster. If the material is very soft, like light straw-clay, long 5 inch staples can be made out of stiff fencing wire. Once the seams are covered, a sticky straw-clay plaster is always the next layer. Thereafter, other layers can be applied as described earlier.

This may be helpful...

Some hesitations about earth bags, tire houses and rammed earth

There are three earthen building techniques that we don't talk much about during our workshops but that people often come across, which each in their own way have a certain appeal: earth bags (sometimes called "super adobe"), rammed tires (most often used for building "earthships") and rammed earth. Many beautiful houses have been created using these techniques, and highly skilled practitioners can be found as well as well written books on each of these subjects. However, they seem to be more popular with people reading about them (non-builders) than with actual builders, who are mostly drawn to some form of cob or adobe brick to create wall systems.

All three of these techniques use forms in the building process, because the earth is kept fairly dry and requires tamping, pounding or ramming in order for the clay-soil to stick together. In the case of earth bags and tires, the forms will stay in the wall, while with rammed earth, wooden forms are built and after the ramming process taken down again.

Earth bag houses have the additional expense of the bags, while rammed earth construction requires a fair bit of dimensional lumber in order to make forms. Tire house builders usually get their "forms" for free as tires are a worldwide waste problem. There are concerns about potential toxic ingredients in and off-gassing from the tires, though.

All forms of earthen construction require moving a significant amount of earth from the ground into the shape of the wall; this is inherently labor intensive. Rammed earth and tire houses are no exception. However, the nature of the work involved in these types of building requires much more tamping and pounding, work that many people find to be unpleasant. In high-end rammed earth houses, the contractor usually uses mechanical tampers to do the job, which is not possible with tires; they need to be pounded one by one, usually with a sledgehammer.

Earth bag houses are sometimes built in a dome shape, where both the walls and the ceiling are made out of the bags. This gives an interesting architectural effect, but usually requires the use of a cement-based plaster to seal the top of the dome against the elements. This can lead to problems with cracking and potential leaking down the road. Rammed earth builders in North America usually add a small percentage of cement to the mix in order to get it code approved. In Morocco, where rammed earth is a popular earthen building technique, cement is usually not added to the mix.

With all three techniques, the presence of forms will limit the ability or speed with which interesting features can be added to the house. Putting in windows and doors becomes more complicated, as do niches, thin walls, and the finishing of the walls. Rammed earth walls can be left "as-is" after the forms are taken off, or they can be plastered. With tires and earth bags however, the shape of the tires/bags add complications and extra work if you want smooth finished walls.

Last but not least, remodels, additions, modifications and repairs are more cumbersome in buildings made with forms. Although we all think that we can build the perfect house in one shot, life often changes and our housing needs become different from the time when we built the house.

Some very beautiful and interesting houses have been constructed using these three techniques. They all take advantage of the abundance of earth by using it as a building material, often extolling the value of the technique in terms of ecological stewardship, ease of building, and potential to inexpensively "house the world". However, considering all the earthen building that takes place worldwide, these techniques are, and will likely remain, fringe methods. If you are interested in building a house using these methods, carefully consider why you would choose to use them.

1.9 Technical Principles of Earthen Construction

Tests

One of the great attractions of earthen construction is the use of local clay-soil. All clay-soils are different, thus it is important to do a test with your soil before you use it in a real project. Make the test representative of the real project; build a little cob wall, plaster a 3' x 3' section of wall, etc. Depending on your experience with and knowledge of the local clay-soil, testing can be scaled back.

Unstabilized earth

All earthen construction techniques described here use some form of un-stabilized earth. The hardening process happens because the materials dry out. This means that if you were to hydrate it again, it would get soft; the materials have not changed chemically. (The one exception is adding cement to the mix for earthbag construction). For earthen building projects to last, they need to be kept relatively dry. Often, a little rain will not hurt it, but continuous water flow will eventually saturate, soften and erode the material.

There are advantages to building with un-stabilized earth. One is that if a crack or blemish shows up, it's very simple to repair by re-moistening the surface and/or applying some fresh material. Often we will leave small cracks alone, as we find that they can actually enhance the character of the building. Another is that un-stabilized earth can be fully recycled into new building materials, or allowed to return to where it came from, the earth!

Don't seal earthen building materials

Earthen plasters, earthen walls, and clay paints are living materials. Small amounts of moisture can be absorbed by the clay particles. This provides excellent humidity control inside the house: when the humidity inside goes up, the clay will absorb moisture. When the humidity is low, the clay can release moisture back to the room. This helps make a room feel very comfortable to live in.

In the case of an earthen house, water vapor can travel through the walls to the outside. Sealing walls with oils, paints, or waxes can hinder this process, causing moisture to get "stuck" inside a wall and eventually cause mold issues. One exception to this is an earthen floor, which is partially sealed with linseed oil. It is very important that the floor is completely dry before you oil it and that no moisture can enter the floor from below.

Also worth mentioning is the use of lime in this context. Water vapor can also move through lime paints and plasters, although not as easily as through earthen materials. Lime adheres well to earthen materials and can be used as a water resistant layer in extremely wet environments. This can include areas where snow may pile-up against a wall, places with wind-driven rain, and bathrooms and saunas. Lime plasters and paints are stabilized, which means they won't become soft again when in contact with water. The drawback of this is that making repairs can be more complicated.

Avoid temperature and moisture extremes

Extreme temperatures during the building process can damage your work. A hard, persistent freeze can make a wet earthen wall or plaster expand and eventually crack. This is less likely to happen if the building is heated. New earthen walls tend to stay wet in the middle for a long time, perhaps as long as a year depending on the climate. The inside and outside surfaces of the wall may be dry, but the middle of the wall likely still holds some moisture from the building process. However, if the building is heated, the heat will slowly travel through the walls toward the outside, taking moisture with it and preventing the walls from freezing and cracking.

Under very wet circumstances, your earthen walls may dry too slowly, hindering progress and potentially enabling mold to grow. Mold on earthen walls is not a problem as long as the wall dries out, effectively depriving the mold of the moisture it needs to reproduce. On plasters, paints, and floors, mold can cause undesirable visible effects. Drying can be greatly enhanced by creating air circulation with the help of electric fans or portable heaters or, if safe to do so, even fires.

Extreme heat combined with direct sunlight can cause finish plasters to dry too quickly, which reduces workability time and can promote cracking. This applies in particular to exterior plasters. Windy conditions can have the same effect. Sometimes simply shading the wall with a tarp can prevent this.

Protect your hands, feet, and lungs

Working with earthen materials day after day can be hard on your hands and feet (if you mix cob barefoot). The clay-soil can be rough, and the clay draws moisture out of your skin. Wearing gloves may be necessary, as well as using moisturizing cream on your hands and feet. When working with dry clay, pigments, and fine sands, try to stand upwind. Clay particles and straw dust, though not toxic, are so small that they can be inhaled, irritating your lungs. Dust masks or bandanas around the nose and mouth are useful.

Screening materials

Hydrating clay

Remember that every technique works because hydrated clay becomes sticky. Therefore, plan ahead and soak your clay or clay-soil before you plan on using it. Even if it soaks for just 15 minutes, it will make your work easier. It is handy to have twice as many buckets on site as you think you may need, using half the buckets to hydrate clay-soil.

Build wet on wet

When adding one earthen material to another, always make sure that the receiving material is moist or dampened. This enables the clay particles to stick and connect. For earthen plasters and clay paints, this may mean dampening the wall with a moist sponge or lightly spraying it with a spray bottle. If a cob wall has dried out, you may need to wet the top with a hose. You can also dunk straw in a bucket of water and put it on top of the wall or simply add a coat of wet clay slip to the wall.

1.10 Earthen building philosophy

Building with earth is about more than just swapping one material for the other. The material embodies a way of building and living that enables us to forgo the damaging, soul-robbing, and expensive consequences of conventional construction.

Slow is fast, fast is slow

Working quickly often slows us down in unexpected ways. The walls of a building may go up faster, but the quality of work may suffer, requiring repairs or rebuilding in the future. It may even lead to dissatisfaction with the project altogether and eventual abandonment. With speed we also tend to hurt ourselves more often. A back injury and visits to the chiropractor can set us back for weeks. Machines can hurt our hearing, cut off fingers, and need constant maintenance. Backhoes and tractors can certainly move earth around very quickly, but may in the process damage trees that have taken decades to grow or compact the soil around a site making it hard for new plants to grow.

It is entirely possible to build large earthen houses with as much speed and expenditure as could be found in the conventional building industry. However, you will then have a conventional house made out of earth. It will lack sculptural design features that were thought of while working slowly by hand. It will have windows put in just a little bit off from where they should be. It will have more milled lumber than natural pieces of round wood. It will look and feel manufactured, rather than hand-built. It will lack the spirit and joy of the builders embedded in the material. Ultimately, it will be short-changed of the love that the builders can make visible. For most people "Building slowly" also means "building yourself;" building by hand at a human speed would be too expensive for most of us if the people doing it were paid by the hour.

Rhythm, routine, and ritual

To make your work joyful and productive, it's better to forgo machines because of their damaging consequences. Instead, think about rhythms, routines, and rituals you might bring into your work.

Rhythms can help make your work easy and light. In building with cob, it is more pleasant and efficient to first mix a substantial amount of material and then build, rather than alternating mixing and building smaller amounts. You'll get into the rhythm of mixing, making each move with less and less effort. In many cultures, earthen building is also accompanied by music. Material gets passed between people and put on the wall to the rhythm of music. This creates speed without hurrying.

Routines can be brought into the organization of the daily schedule: when and where you eat, take breaks, and sharpen and clean tools.

Rituals can include starting the day with a short meditation or song or ending the day with reviewing what you have accomplished and giving thanks.

Build together

Although the mechanization of earthen construction can allow one person to work by themselves, earthen building really lends itself to building in community, using the coordinated movement of many arms and legs to accomplish a lot with seemingly little effort. No extraordinary strength or technical skills are necessary, allowing young and old to participate. Building in community allows people to be part of something greater than themselves. It opens opportunities for creating something beautiful with others, which does not happen very often these days.

Earthen building projects tend to attract people who want to help. I think there are many reasons for this, but three in particular:
- It looks like a fun and easy thing to do; people are having a good time.
- We don't have a negative association with earthen construction. We were never taught in school that we can't do it or only men or professionals can do it. We were never tested on it or manipulated to do it. It does not fit into monetary paradigms.
- Our biological memory and collective consciousness is integrally connected with clay as a material. Because clay is everywhere, and building with clay (as well as pottery) is universal and timeless, we are drawn intuitively towards building with earth. It immediately feels right.

Building as health-giving

By following the suggestions described above, we are not too far off from making the building process health-giving instead of health-robbing. Being outside, working with clay and other natural materials, and enjoying working with others increases one's health and spirit. We can then start looking at how we can make all movements and actions light and enjoyable. Two half full buckets are easier to carry than one full one. Working barefoot stimulates pressure points on the soles of our feet. Our spinal column is constantly in motion, helping us avert back pain. Building can do the same things for us as gardening, swimming, and hiking: it can make us stronger, healthier, and happier.

Understanding how to live with earthen buildings

People are often concerned that earthen buildings will deteriorate quickly or wash away in the rain. Our experience has shown that if they are well built and well protected from the elements, they will last just as long as conventionally built houses. Furthermore, as earthen materials change over time (cracks develop, plasters wear, rain changes the surface) they actually get more beautiful, like a well-loved pair of blue jeans. Conversely, conventional building materials tend to look worse over time. This represents well the idea that aging is different from deteriorating. Finally, if repairs are needed, they are typically easier and less expensive with earthen materials. You won't need to call a specialist to come and fix a plaster crack or re-finish a damaged floor; you can do it yourself with the materials, tools and knowledge you have on-hand.

This may be helpful...

Building together with your community

Many people dream about being part of a community where people help each other out with various aspects of daily living, like cooking, cleaning, gardening, and even building houses. Because building with earth is relatively easy and forgiving and benefits from the work of many hands and feet, it would seem ideally suited for such an approach. And it is! However, people often underestimate how delicate the process of working in community can be.

We often hear of stories of people who were confident that their friends would show up for a weekend of helping out, and then had them not show up at all. In order to build in community, you need to have a community, and that is easier said than done. Building a house may be a tricky choice for a first community building activity.

Having said so, many groups of people have had a great time building together for a day or a week. Here are a few tips that can make this happen for you:

Easy does it. Make sure that there are enough simple, repetitive tasks for those who want to help. Sifting clay-soil, moving sand, mixing cob, etc. The simpler the tasks, the more people have a chance to connect, chat, look around, observe, and participate.

Clear communication. Communicate when you will start (and end) the workday, what people should bring, what is provided (food, coffee, other drinks, work gloves?).

Food, drink and music. Almost inevitably, people open themselves up to connecting with others under the influence of good food, good drinks and good music! It's important to use this to your advantage. Even the simple promise of pizza and beer at the end of the day can make a huge difference. Ensure a good quality boombox with some easy to follow music. Strong rhythms are important!

Value your community. Be clear about your needs and share them with the people that want to help. Tell them you are counting on them and show your sincere gratitude.

Offer a learning experience. A work party, with some work and preparation, can also morph into a one-day workshop or course. Show some slides, discuss some issues, teach some additional techniques.

Fun and games. People love to play and laugh but are often not allowed to (or don't allow themselves to). Provide opportunities and openings for play, jokes, and humor. Play some group games, or just promote a degree of playfulness on the worksite.

Let people shine. Ask your community about who they are, or give them a chance to express themselves in a group break. Everyone is interesting. If you want to appreciate someone, get to know him or her.

Don't give up. Maybe, the first time you organize a work party only one person will show up. Make sure the two of you have a great time and relish the opportunity to get to know this person. Build on the success of the first day and try to get 2 people the next week. Building community takes time.

Part 2:
The building techniques

2.1 Building with cob

Visit <u>www.HouseAlive.org</u> for pictures and videos on this chapter.

There are three important elements involved in building with cob: mixing the cob material, building a basic structural wall, and integrating things such as wires, pipes, doors, and windows into the wall.

Mixing cob

For centuries people mixed cob with their hands and feet in a shallow pit. Animals were also used to stomp a muddy mixture of clay-soil and straw. Today we often use human power and a regular old blue poly tarp to efficiently mix cob.

After you have determined your ratio of sand to clay-soil with tests, it's time to mix the cob. There are many ways to mix cob, and everyone will develop a technique that works best for them. The following are three techniques that we teach in our workshops.

<u>**The Canadian Method**</u>: how to mix without getting your feet muddy.
- Lay a 6' x 8' tarp on the ground
- Empty a bucket of sand on the tarp and spread it out a little with your foot.
- Add a bucket of moist or hydrated clay-soil and spread it out on top of the sand with your foot (this assumes a 1:1 ratio).
- Have two people pick up the corners of the tarp on the shorter sides, wrap the corners one time around each hand and stand two to three feet apart.

Mixing "Canadian style"

- Each person will take turns stepping forward with alternating legs onto the tarp and material. When stomping with the right leg, start by lifting up the tarp with your right arm and right knee. This will create a turning action right before you stomp.
- Add water as needed to get the mixture to a well mixed, wet but solid consistency. The material will soon start to sound squishy and will look homogeneous.
- Add straw to the mix, about two handfuls at a time. Do this two or three times or until the mix becomes dryer and stiff like bread dough.
- When you no longer see changes to the material, stop mixing. Don't mix more than necessary as this wastes energy.

Mixing barefoot

Mixing cob barefoot can be an enjoyable and playful way to work. It stimulates the nerve ends on the soles of your feet and creates natural movement in your spine. Through experiencing the materials with your feet you will quickly learn when the cob is mixed well.

When mixing with two people, one person stomps (with bare feet) the mix in the middle of the tarp, while the other person turns it over by moving from corner to corner and flipping the pile. To flip the mix over, stand at the corner of the tarp facing the middle. Grasp the corner and lift up; in one smooth motion, put your knee into the tarp now hanging in front of you, and step onto the pile. The effect is almost like folding the pile of material in half. To keep the cob from moving to the edge of the tarp, move to the next corner before flipping it again. The person stomping the pile in the middle will be flattening out the mix with their feet. For extra mixing effect, they can try making a twisting motion with their hips ("twist and shout") while using their legs and feet like egg beaters. In essence, the two people work in opposition: the person on the outside of the tarp is trying to pile up the mix, while the person in the middle is working to flatten it out.

Mixing alone

If no mixing partner is available, either method can also be done alone. For the Canadian method, put the initial buckets of materials on one end of the tarp and use your lift-knee-stomp action to move it to the other end. Then walk to the other side and repeat. For barefoot mixing, flatten out the pile with your feet, then bend over, grab a corner, and pull the material back into a pile again.

Good cob, bad cob?

Over time you will learn what the qualities of the mix that best suits your purposes are. To help you learn to recognize when your mix is ready, here are some tips:

- You should be able to throw a loaf-size amount (called a "cob") to someone 10 feet away without it falling apart. If it does fall apart, the mix is likely low on clay and so you may need to increase the ratio of clay-soil to sand.

- If it seems very sticky, you may want to add some more sand to the mix. Too much clay can cause cracking in the walls as they dry. The more straw you put in the mix, the stronger the walls will be.
- Straw will also help during the building process, allowing you to build higher in one building session without the wet walls bulging out.
- Under damp and cold conditions, mix relatively dry batches of cob and add a lot of straw to the mix. Otherwise, the walls will become too wet and weak to continue building.
- Too much straw will make the cob very labor intensive to mix and build or do sculptural work with. Experiment to find the right amount of straw for your mix.

Things to remember:
- Don't sweat the recipe; the margins of acceptable cob are very wide. Relax, drink lots of water, and dance. You are doing what humankind has done for millennia. Trust your senses!
- Making wet batches of cob is easier. However, wet cob makes it harder to build the wall up high in one building session. This also depends on how fast the walls dry, which in turn depends on wind, humidity, and temperature. You can play with timing, for example, by mixing wet cob before lunch, letting it stiffen up during lunch, and then building with it after lunch. You could even mix cob one day, to build with the following day.
- Carrying two half buckets is always easier than one full bucket and much better for your back as well. You can even invest in some smaller buckets to make sure you stick to that idea. When moving buckets or batches of cob, consider the use of a hand-truck or dolly. They are easier to use than wheelbarrows because you don't have to lift buckets off the ground. They also take up less space on the building site.
- Most people prefer to mix for about an hour and then build with that material until it's all used up. This allows you to stay in the rhythm of an activity and for the wall to set and dry a bit while you're mixing. It's better not to mix after a meal or when it's very hot. Early morning and late afternoon tend to be the best times.
- Think about organizing your mixing site efficiently and comfortably. Is it on flat ground? Is it in the shade? How far is it from your piles of clay-soil and sand and how far is it from the building site?
- Playing live or recorded music during the mixing process can help a lot. If you have an uneven number of people and one of them is a talented musician, let that person create a beat to work to. Whatever music you use, make sure that it has an easily recognizable beat. Too folksy or wild-and-crazy will not work for everyone.

Water management:
- To add water to the mix, use a bucket rather than a hose. It's faster, more accurate, and easier if you are building with a group. (You don't have to search or wait for the hose.)
- Fill your water bucket from a larger tub of water (a trash can works well). Make filling up the tub part of the morning or evening routine. The use of hoses will increase the

risk of water spilling on the mixing site, potentially creating a muddy "slip 'n slide" scene.
- Wash your hands, feet, and tools in buckets of water that can be reused as water for cob mixing.

Stockpiling wet cob:
- Stockpile your cob as close to your building site as you can. This may mean having several piles around a project.
- Always pile cob on a tarp and cover it with another tarp if you think it will dry out too much before you are ready to build with it.
- Do not put cob too close to the wall you are working on; there should be enough space between the pile and the wall for you to work comfortably, perhaps as much as three feet.
- Don't stand or walk on a pile of cob; it will become compacted and harder to pull apart.
- If stockpiled cob has dried out too much, it becomes too hard to build with. The straw and clay will dry out the mix as they continue to absorb water while the cob is stored. You can remix it with a little water. This can go very quickly and is well worth it.
- When it's really hot, pour some water and put some wet straw on a pile of cob and cover it with two tarps, slowing the drying process.

Mixing cob with machines

Many people have successfully mixed cob with mortar mixers, cement mixers and tractor-like devices. Sometimes this can speed things up, sometimes this will slow you down. It does bring fumes, danger and noise to the building site and makes it less inviting to build as a community. When cob gets mixed fast, it needs to go on the wall fast as well, which undoubtedly lead to a lesser quality building. When considering bringing machines, make sure you take into account the cleaning and maintaining of them as part of the equation; cob can be very taxing on equipment.

Building with cob

When building cob walls, you add wet blobs of cob to the previous layer, which ideally is still somewhat wet and mushy, making it easy to integrate the new material. Here are a few important strategies to help you build beautiful walls.

- When building with others, work in pairs. One person delivers the cob, the other builds. It is very inefficient for one person to walk back and forth to get their own cob. Deliver the cob to the builder in as large a blob as possible. Don't worry about shaping it nicely as long as it stays together in the handing over or throwing. Sometimes one delivery person can supply two builders.

- Build from the edges of the wall towards the middle of the wall. When you start this way, the wall will look like a gentle V with the low point in the middle of the wall. People have a tendency to start in the middle, creating an upside down V, which is sometimes referred to as shouldering. This creates a slope that is harder to build on. As you work toward the middle of the wall, fill in the V and shape the wall like a box: flat on the top with vertical sides.

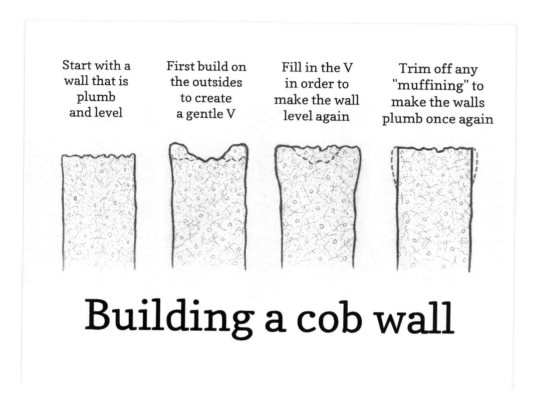

Start with a wall that is plumb and level

First build on the outsides to create a gentle V

Fill in the V in order to make the wall level again

Trim off any "muffining" to make the walls plumb once again

Building a cob wall

- Use your fingers and thumbs to integrate fresh cob into the wall. It needs to be integrated to the point where you can't lift off the cob you have just added.
- Only apply pressure to a wet wall straight down. Putting pressure on the side, especially if the wall is high, can cause the wall to wobble and maybe even crack and fall over. If you need to apply some material to the side to correct something, use your other arm or hand on the opposite side of the wall to compensate for any sideways pressure.
- When building on the outside edges of the wall, use one hand as a movable form, helping you keep the wall going up plumb.
- Except for when the wall is very low, do not reach across the wall to build on the side that is on the opposite side from where you are standing; it is hard to see what you're doing. Have someone else work on the other side of the wall. If you are

building alone, complete one side and then walk around the wall to work on the other side. This will make it a lot easier to keep the walls plumb.

- If the wall is higher than your belly button, use a scaffold, ladder or straw bales to get higher up. Building above your belly button is much more physically challenging as you can't use the weight of your upper body to knead the fresh cob into the wall. Additionally, it becomes more difficult to see what you are doing.
- End building sessions with a four-inch spine over the center of the wall, with ribs coming off that spine about every six inches. This will facilitate drying because more cob surface is exposed to the air. If you have to take an extended break from building, the spine and rib method will give you some good teeth for when you start building again on the dry wall.

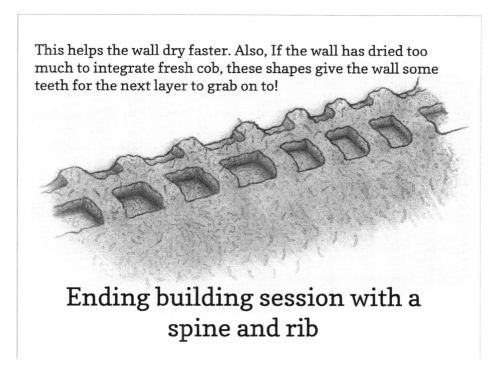

This helps the wall dry faster. Also, If the wall has dried too much to integrate fresh cob, these shapes give the wall some teeth for the next layer to grab on to!

Ending building session with a spine and rib

- Under poor drying conditions, you can also use a stick to poke holes in the wall, about 3/4 inch wide, one inch apart and one inch deep. This will expose more wall surface to the air and will increase evaporation. Find a comfortable stick or dowel as a tool to do this.

Trimming cob
It is hard, if not impossible, to build perfectly plumb walls with your hands. There are two reasons for this:

1. We cannot estimate perfect plumb with our eyes, and

2. Because of the weight of wet cob on top, the fresh material right below the top tends to bulge out before it has a chance to dry. The more straw in the cob and the drier the mix, the less this will happen.

As much as we like organically shaped walls, they do need to go up plumb. If not, there is a great risk of the wall falling over in the building process. Even if they don't fall, irregular or "leaning" walls are uncomfortable to look at and live with.

Always use a level (at least 4' long) and an old handsaw or machete to trim the wall. The cob comes off easier if it has had a chance to set up a bit. In very dry, warm, or windy conditions, make sure you don't wait too long to trim. It's a lot more labor intensive to fix a non-plumb wall once the cob has completely dried out.

The bulging of the top of the wall, which we call "muffining" is a normal occurrence. Most of the time we find that the building process is a constant routine of putting cob on the wall, mixing more cob, and then correcting the last layer with a level and saw. We actually welcome a little bit of muffining as this allows us to shape the wall with a saw, rather than trying to build the wall perfectly with our hands.

Cob connections
Buildings are more than just walls. There are many other features and elements that must be integrated into a comfortable house. The most common ones are:

- Windows
- Doors
- Roofs
- Plumbing pipes
- Electrical wires
- Things hanging from the wall, such as cabinets, paintings, etc.
- Shelving built into the wall

Windows
There are two types of windows: ones that can open, and ones that have fixed panes of glass (non-openable). For either type, the windows themselves are only put in, after the walls have been built and are dry or nearly dry.

Openable windows:

- Build a 2 x 6 (or similar) wooden frame that will be the right size for the window to fit into, with about a ¼" of space all around between the window and the frame. Brace the corners so that the frame will stay square. On the outside part of the frame, nail a

2 x 2 (or something like it) on the vertical side, around which the cob can be built. This is what keeps the window frame in place: it forms a "tooth" in the cob.

- Put the frame on the cob wall. It does not have to be parallel to the wall; you can angle it a little to let more sun in or to facilitate a view. You can also move it toward the inside or outside of the wall, depending on how big you want your inside and outside windowsills to be. More often than not, it is best to put the window toward the outside of the wall: this will create a larger indoor windowsill and provides less of a ledge on the outside for rain to collect. Level and plumb the frame and brace it to the ground with long poles or lumber. This will ensure that the window frame stays in place and plumb while the walls are going up. Check and correct this as necessary while the walls go up.
- Build the cob walls up about two inches above the top of the window frame. Then bridge the walls on either side of the frame with wood, which is called a header, on top of which you can continue building with cob. For each foot of span, use at least a one-inch thick layer of wood. Near corners or where roof rafters land on the header, double the thickness of the header. Any wood can be used or combined. You can make your own beams by nailing pieces of wood together. Make sure the header spans the full width of the wall.
- The two-inch gap between the window frame and the header ensures that as the building settles and the clay shrinks, the window frame won't get crushed or deformed by the weight above it. Once the building is dry, use a combination of hardware cloth and straw-clay plaster to fill and finish that area. The 2 x 6 frame can be finished with a nice wooden trim or with straw-clay plaster and a finish plaster. For insulation purposes make sure to use plenty of straw to fill in any gaps around the window frame.

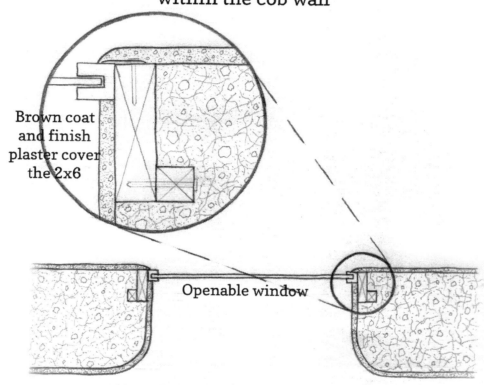

2x6 frame with a 2x2 attached,
so tame can't move
within the cob wall

Brown coat
and finish
plaster cover
the 2x6

Openable window

Putting an openable window in a cob wall

Unopenable ("fixed") windows:

This is where we take a pane of glass and stick it in the cob wall. Dual pane glass is recommended for houses that will require heating. Contrary to popular belief, it is not a good idea to just stick panes of glass in the wet cob as you are building; they often break due to settling and drying of the cob. Here is how to do it:

- Measure the outside dimensions of the glass and build a 2 x 4 or 2 x 6 frame that is one inch larger all around on the outside of the frame. Brace the corners so they will remain square.
- Put the frame on the wall and brace it to the ground, as with openable windows. Do not attach a "tooth" on the outside of the frame, as you will take this frame out later. The frame functions as a placeholder!
- Build the walls up around the frame. Do not build cob on the face of the frame that is facing in the direction from which you will later remove the frame, which is usually the outside. As with openable windows, build the walls about two inches above the frame before you put in a header.
- Once the walls are dry, take out the braces, pop out the frame, and put in the window pane in its place. Secure it with straw-clay plaster.
- The gap above the window can also be filled with straw-clay plaster.
- If you wish, you can now give the window any shape you want by sculpting with cob and/or straw-clay plaster on the inside and/or outside of the window. Straw-clay plaster sticks well to glass!

Doors

As with windows, it is best to mimic conventional construction techniques by building a rough frame in which you later build a door. This could be a homemade or conventional pre-hung door, or you could hang a door directly to the rough frame. This last option may seem easier, but in the end it will more likely result in air leaks and problematic closure.

The rough frame can be attached to the cob in different ways. You could add a 2 x 2 to each vertical outside face of the frame, creating "teeth" that the cob will mold around. Or you can install dead-men into the cob as the wall goes. This is a bulky piece of wood that butts up against the door frame and gets completely imbedded into the cob wall. Install at least three on each side of the frame, evenly spaced. With a pencil, mark on the inside of the frame where the dead-men are located. Once the cob is dry, screw the door frame into the dead-men. Don't do this before the walls are dry as the building will settle and might pull out or bend the screws.

It is best if the dead-men are embedded in the middle of the cob wall. If your door frame is all the way on the outside of the wall, cut the dead-men at a slight angle so they will face toward the center of the wall.

In both cases the frame needs to be temporarily braced from the top of the frame to the ground. This ensures the frame remains plumb. A header can be installed two inches above the door frame, and once the building is dry, the whole area can be finished as described above for windows.

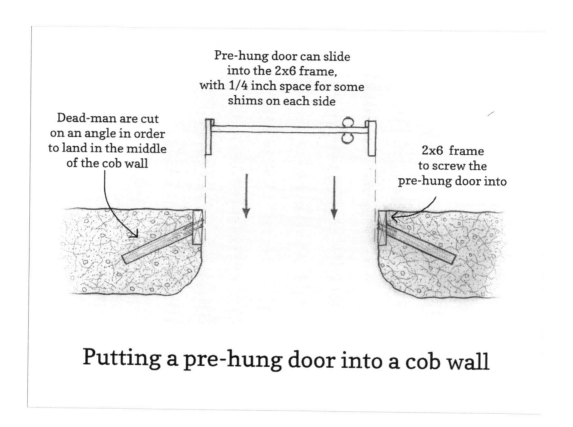

Pre-hung door can slide into the 2x6 frame, with 1/4 inch space for some shims on each side

Dead-man are cut on an angle in order to land in the middle of the cob wall

2x6 frame to screw the pre-hung door into

Putting a pre-hung door into a cob wall

Roofs

Roofs are connected to cob walls by embedding rafter anchors at least a foot below the top of the cob wall. These roof anchors can be pieces of wood, cable, strong wire, or metal straps. It is important that they have some resistance in the cob so when a strong wind pulls on the roof, the anchor does not slide out of the wall. Cables and wires can be wrapped and nailed around small blocks of wood and buried in the wall. Wooden anchors can be installed at angles so they can not lift straight out of the cob. Nails sticking out of the wood also create extra resistance.

If you are not sure where the rafters will end up landing on the wall, you can still put in the anchors. Put in more than you will need and use the ones that end up close to where the roof rafters end up landing. In rectangular shaped buildings you can use the anchors to attach a top plate, on which you can then attach your roof rafters. Once enough anchors are deeply embedded in the cob, the wind will have a hard time blowing your roof away!

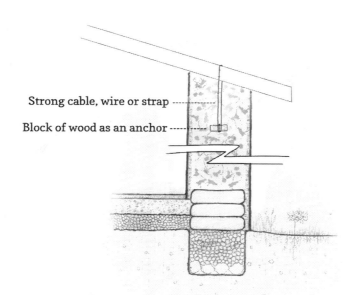

Strong cable, wire or strap ⋯⋯⋯

Block of wood as an anchor ⋯⋯⋯

Roof rafter attachment to cob wall

Plumbing

A leak in any building is a bummer when water pipes are buried inside the wall, whether it is cob or a conventional building. Hence, the following suggestions:

- Use flexible poly-pipe for water supply lines (brands are called PEX and Wirsbo). It is much stronger and more flexible than copper or PVC.
- With poly pipe you can avoid having connections inside a wall because it is flexible enough to go around corners. Plumbing connections are usually the places where leaks happen.
- Lay your pipe well inside the wall. On exterior walls in areas with hard freezes, put the pipes closer to the inside of the building, however, not closer than two inches from the inside, so as to avoid accidentally puncturing them with a nail or screw.
- Unpressurized grey-water pipes can go anywhere in the cob. It is always better to avoid connections within a cob wall.
- While walls go up, you can install "sleeves" in the wall to become spaces through which pipes or wires can later be brought into the house. Use scrap pieces of pipe

that are larger than the actual pipes or wires you plan to put through the sleeves. Once you have brought the pipe into your house, fill the space in the sleeve with cob, straw-clay plaster, or some combination of the two. You can even slightly angle the pipe towards the outside so that if a leak does occur it will less likely affect the inside of the building.

Electrical wires and boxes

Romex wires can be put directly in the middle of cob walls as the walls go up. The direct burial type (usually grey) is much stronger but a little harder to work with and is also more expensive. Make sure that wires are not too close to the edge of the wall to avoid an accidental puncture by a nail or screw. For larger buildings with more complex wiring, it is easier to wait until the walls are finished and then cut a three-inch deep groove in the wall to insert the wires into. You can use "side walk chalk" to map out the wiring. The best time to do this is when the walls are still somewhat soft. As an alternative to Romex, you can use conduit, which is also best put in after the walls have been built.

Either way, the wires will have to connect to electrical boxes. While the walls go up, place blocks of wood a bit larger than the boxes you plan to use in the spots where you want the electrical boxes to be. Once the walls are trimmed and almost dry, take out the wooden blocks and replace them with the electrical boxes. The easiest way to secure a box to the wall is to put a few screws in the side of the box, about two on each side, and lead the wire through the back of the box. Then set the whole unit into the hole in the wall and fill the space around the box with wet cob. Make sure the box sticks out far enough so that the outside of the box will be flush with the finish plaster.

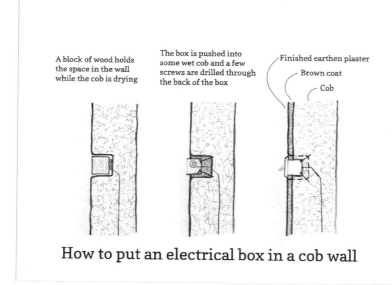

How to put an electrical box in a cob wall

If your wall is completely dried out and you need to cut a groove for wires or pipes, wet the wall over the course of a few hours with a sprayer. This will make chipping the wall a lot easier. Continue wetting the wall as your groove gets deeper. An angle grinder with a masonry blade will also do the job but is very unpleasant and dangerous to use.

Hanging things on the walls

Paintings and pictures can easily be hung on cob walls with a two inch or longer screw. If you have heavy items and are worried about them falling off the wall, you can do the following:

- Drill a 1 1/2 inch diameter hole in the wall about four inches deep. Make sure you don't hit any wires or pipes. Count on any drill bit being dulled by the cob, so use one you are willing to ruin.
- Stick a wooden dowel or piece of wood in the hole.
- Tightly fill whatever space is left with wood shims or splinters, followed by wet cob.
- Let it dry and cut it flush with the finished wall surface. You can nail or screw a fastener into this piece of wood to hang whatever you want. It will never come down.
- For cabinets connect several of these dowels with a 1 x 4 wooden plate. You will then have lots of options for hanging cabinets. It's preferable to have the surface of the wooden plate be flush with the finish wall, so either install it before you apply the brown coat, or carve out a groove in the finish coat for it set into.

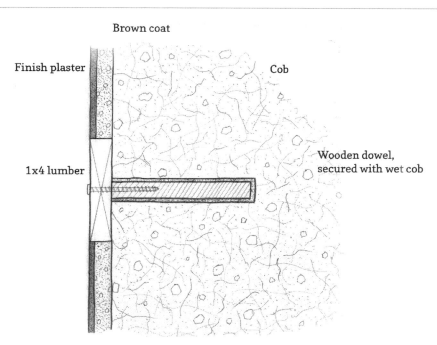

Preparing a cob wall for hanging heavy things from it

Shelves and niches

It is easy to take wooden planks and build them directly into the cob wall to create shelves. For example:

- If the wall is 18" wide, you can take a 2' section and just make it 12" wide, with a 6" space left open on the inside. The wall will become a little weaker because of this. Do not make exterior load bearing walls any thinner than 12".
- Go as high as you want the shelves to go and then bridge the gap in the wall with a header, 1" thick for every foot of span.
- Now, decide where you want the shelves to go. Use a level and make scratch marks in the wall at the different levels. Using an old screwdriver, crow bar or small piece of wood, carve out grooves in which the wooden shelves can later slide. The grooves should be about twice as thick as the thickness of the shelves. Do not put the shelves in at this point! The wall may still settle, almost guaranteeing that the shelves will end up not being level.
- Cut the wooden shelves so that they are the right length to slide into the grooves. They can also be a bit wider than the 6" indent in the wall, so that they protrude a few inches into the room.
- Wait until the building is dry and then slide the shelves into the grooves. Fill in the space in the grooves with a little cob above and below the shelves, using a level to ensure that the shelf is in a level position.

If you make just a tiny shelf or "niche" (no wider than 10", or deeper than 4"), it is often easier to just carve the space out of the wall after the wall has been built, but while it is still somewhat soft. In this case you usually won't have to put in a header because the cob above is already stable enough. You can choose to carve the top of such a little niche in the shape of a decorative arch.

Anytime you want to build an arch in a cob wall that is wider than a foot, you are better off building a simple form out of stiff wire mesh or flexible wood. Arches may be appropriate for shelves or niches carved into walls, or for creating an arched window opening. Assuming your window is all the way on the outside of the wall, you can form your arch on the inside of the wall and then stick a straw-clay plaster to the glass on the outside of the wall, which mimics the shape of the arch on the inside.

This may be helpful...

How long does it take to build with earth

Often, when discussing the pros and cons of building with earthen materials, it is brought up that it is such a labor-intensive way of building. It is valuable to look at this statement carefully and see what it suggests about who we are as a culture in relation to work, time and building.

My parents taught me that doing physical labor was something to be left for poor and/ or uneducated people. In other words, "you better do well in school, otherwise you may be stuck digging ditches for the rest of your life." A life of farming, road building, coal mining or truck driving was simply not a reasonable option for me, according to my parents. In some ways, I think they were right: there are a lot of demeaning, damaging, monotonous jobs out there, that I'd rather not do for a living. However, it also instilled in me the general principle that "doing physical labor" is something to be avoided.

But what if the labor becomes so pleasurable, so health giving, so rhythmic, so full of joy and empowerment that you actually want to do it? "Labor intensive" would then be considered a positive statement. Why would you want to do less of something you enjoy? This is the overwhelming experience of people who build with earthen materials, assuming they have given themselves enough time to build by hand and foot.

Our obsession with speed and getting things done gets in the way of us fully living our lives. Why? Because in reality, we will never be done with our work. Once your house is done you will move on to the next thing that needs to get done. The thought that we need to "get it done" suggests that we want to get our work over with because it is unpleasant. But if it's enjoyed, the time spent making a beautiful house is time well spent!

Aside from these philosophical considerations, it is helpful to look at the practicality of building by hand and foot. By harvesting and processing our own building materials, we do the work which the lumber mill (and scores of other factories) does for the conventional builder (at a price). If those builders had to go out into the woods and make their own 2x6 lumber from standing trees, building with earthen materials may not seem so labor intensive in comparison. Many earthen builders enjoy having time rather than money, and use that time to hand-build their house.

Once we accept that it is ok for the building process to take time, it is more likely that the house will be "crafted", rather than "assembled" (or stapled and glued together) as is the case with conventional building. Consequently, earthen houses tend to be more creative, beautiful, and cared for. Craftsmanship in the conventional building world comes at a high price; with earthen construction techniques, especially with cob, novice builders can be craftspeople as the wall goes up.

The "de-industrialization" of the building process also means that we can pay closer attention to the impact we have on the earth. The harvesting of materials can be done locally and carefully and with very little waste. The labor-intensive methods become a key part of promoting sustainability and care for the earth.

Lastly, remember that many hands make light work. Often people imagine that they are alone in the world and therefore have to be able to do everything by themselves. This is a choice, but it doesn't have to be that way. Building with earth is an invitation for people to connect with one another by building together.

So, the stigma that the term "labor intensive" has, may not serve us well. Perhaps we should seek out activities and crafts that are more labor intensive, rather than less. Labor can bring us health, beauty and community and reduce our dependency on oil and industry and money. Of course, with enough machines and diesel fuel, I can put together any size earthen house in the same time as the conventional builder assembles his or hers together. But why would I?

2.2 Wood-cob, rock-cob and Bale-cob

Visit www.HouseAlive.org for pictures and videos on this chapter.

Because of the strength of cob and its ability to take on any shape, it is possible to put things in the cob that take up space and reduce the total amount of cob needed. This can have advantages for the building process and aesthetics of the wall, as well as improve the performance of the building.

Wood-cob

Wood rounds, split firewood, scraps of lumber, or other junk pieces of wood can be stuck in the cob during the building process. To prepare the wood, make sure that it is not just dry, but seasoned, meaning that most of the moisture has left the wood. For freshly cut trees this could take as long as two years, depending on your climate. (Often, you can purchase seasoned firewood). This will ensure the wood will not shrink and create weaknesses inside the wall. Make sure that the bark is off the wood and that the wood is free from insects, and cut them in lengths that equal the width of the wall.

To maintain the integrity of the cob, build at least two inches of cob around each piece of wood, and avoid stacking one piece directly on top of another. Each piece should be placed so that it is in between two pieces in the row below. This way the cob will take on the shape of a honeycomb, which has a lot of structural integrity.

The biggest advantage of putting wood in the cob is that you can build faster, because less cob mixing is required. Wood cut to the exact width of the wall will also make it easier to raise the wall plumb. Very little trimming will be needed, and the wall won't have a tendency to "muffin." However, time saved on the building site may approximate time spent acquiring and preparing the wood.

Because wood is a better insulator than cob, your walls will have less mass but more insulation. This may be an advantage in colder climates or on colder sides of the house. You may also choose to leave one or both faces of the wood exposed, to create a visual effect. In that case you have to cut the wood long enough so that it will be flush with the finished wall. Any wood that is exposed on the outside of a building is vulnerable and needs to be treated. On the inside of the wall, it helps to sand the wood nicely and then oil it. Having all that wood in the wall will certainly make it easier to find a place for nails or screws for attaching cabinets or hanging pictures. However, it could complicate the installation of water lines and electricity wires.

If you plan on leaving the wood exposed, realize that plastering around exposed wood is labor intensive. Covering the wood up with an earthen plaster will make it fairly simple to finish the wall. It's easiest to use a straw-clay plaster that can be applied as a brown coat over the whole wall. After that you can apply a finish coat as you would with any earthen wall. Once the wood is covered with these materials, it won't be susceptible to rot or insects anymore. (Note: In some tropical climates, termites can dig into the cob and find the wood.)

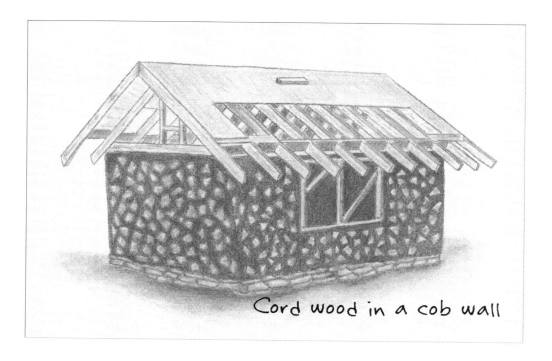

Cord wood in a cob wall

Rock-cob

Many of the whitewashed villages in southern Spain were built by mortaring stones together with a cob-like material. After that they would use a "lime wash" (paint made out of lime) to protect the wall from rain and to keep them cool in the summer. Similarly, we have often put rocks into cob walls, sometimes simply because they were laying around, or perhaps to speed up the building process. In poor drying conditions, this is a great way to get a lift on your wall without it muffining too much. When putting rocks (or any other solid objects) in a cob wall, use the same principles as described for wood cob: build a honeycomb of cob around each rock (or object), with at least 2 inches in between the rocks. The faces of rocks can be left exposed on the inside or the outside of the wall for an aesthetic touch. Be aware that rocks are much denser than cob and will make your house heavier and make the walls less insulative.

Bale-cob

Because most straw bales are very compressed, they won't create instability if you replace a section of cob with a bale. To make this possible, the cob wall has to be at least the width of a bale, either flat or on its side. It is also safest to have at least two feet of solid cob on either side of the bale.

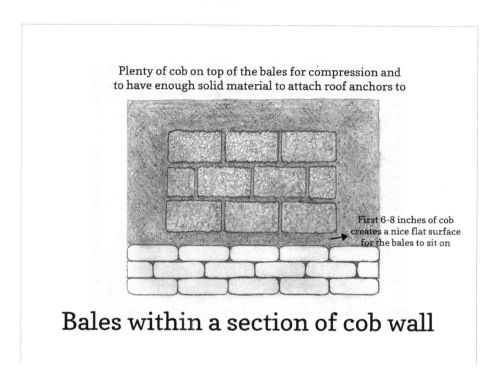

Plenty of cob on top of the bales for compression and to have enough solid material to attach roof anchors to

First 6-8 inches of cob creates a nice flat surface for the bales to sit on

Bales within a section of cob wall

Before you place a bale, apply clay slip on the top and bottom of the bale. It's easiest to do that with your hands (and gloves). Then put it on the wall and start cobbing around it. For extra strength you can drive two wooden or bamboo stakes through the bale into the cob below the bale. (Be aware of wires and pipes in the cob). For finishing the bales, the first earthen layer on a bale needs to be a straw-clay plaster. It helps to first brush the bales with a clay-slip.

If your building design calls for a long straight wall with no windows or doors, as is often the case on the northern side of a building, you can fill a whole section with bales. In addition to greatly reducing the amount of cob you need to mix, this will make for a wall that is much better insulated on the side of the house where you may need it most. It's not clear what the maximum size section is that you can comfortably build with bales, but excellent results have been achieved by lining up three bales and building three rows high. This will give you a section of wall approximately ten feet long and four feet high that can be built in just a few hours.

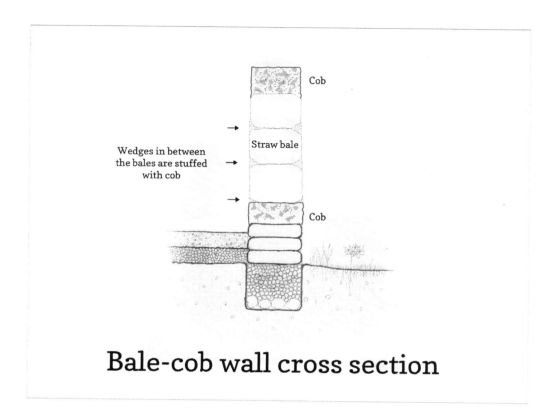

Cob

Straw bale

Wedges in between
the bales are stuffed
with cob

Cob

Bale-cob wall cross section

When putting in several rows of bales, it's easier to first build the cob up on either side of where the bales will go. Then:

· Coat the top and bottom of the first layer of bales with slip and put them into the wall. Make sure they fit very tightly in the space between the cob walls! They should be compressed but not so much that they buckle out. Make smaller bales as needed. (First sew a new piece of baling twine through the bale and tie it off before you cut the strings; otherwise, the bale will expand beyond repair.)
· Pin these bales to the cob below with bamboo or wooden stakes.
· Build the next rows in the same way. Pin each row to the bales below. Make sure the bales are stacked without any vertical seams. If your first row was made of three whole bales, start the next row with a half-bale at the ends and two full bales in the middle. The row after that can be three whole bales again.
· Now is a good time to stuff any wires or pipes in between the bales as needed.
· Once all the bales are stacked, fill all the seams and gaps with as much cob as you can, all the way into the center of the wall if possible. This will help compress and stabilize each individual bale. You are using wet cob to chink the bales. Don't use so much cob that the bales start to shift.
· Put at least another foot, but not more than 2 feet, of cob on top of the bales before adding anything like roof rafters, a top plate, or windows. This extra weight will help compress the bales.

• Now you are ready to brown coat the wall with a straw-clay plaster.
Even after the wall has dried, the intersection between the cob and the straw bale may be a place where minor cracking occurs in the finish earthen plaster.

One of the interesting things about bale-cob is that the walls are stable and strong from the moment you chink the bales with cob, even before the cob dries. A combination of things contribute to this: the tight fit of the bales, the use of clay slip as a glue, the pinning, the chinking, and the weight of a foot of cob (or more) on top. Even building three feet of cob on top of a bale wall built in this way has not caused any problems.

This may be helpful…

How earthen buildings moderate

Earthen buildings have many advantages over conventional buildings made out of wood, stone, concrete or brick. One great advantage is the moderating effect that earthen walls have on temperature swings, humidity, and sound. These qualities can have a major influence on whether we feel good in a certain space.

Because of the weight (mass) of earthen buildings, the interior temperature tends to change only at a very slow rate. Once the walls are warmed up, they tends to stay warm for a long time, sometimes days, even though it is cold outside and not much heat is being created inside the building. Likewise, on hot summer days, the mass soaks up the heat, keeping the air fresh and cool on the inside. The constant temperature of earthen buildings helps us to feel very comfortable. While our bodies can adjust to different temperatures, dramatic fluctuations have more of an impact on us, which is why the constant temperature of earthen buildings make us feel so comfortable. One can understand this mechanism through the experience of shifting through seasons: the first hot day of summer feels a lot hotter than a day with exactly the same temperature toward the end of the summer, when our bodies have adjusted to the heat.

Just as the mass of an earthen wall moderates temperature fluctuations, so does the clay moderate the humidity in a space. Clay has a capacity to absorb and release moisture, dehumidifying a room when it is humid and adding moisture when the air is dry. In really hot and dry climates this helps keep the inside of the house feeling fresh and pleasant (by increasing the humidity), while in hot and humid climates, it helps keep the indoor humidity a little lower, making the heat more bearable. Cold winter air tends to be much dryer, and people commonly experience very dry indoor air during the winter. Clay walls can help raise the humidity level inside, reducing the potential for chapped lips and static electricity!

Finally, because the earthen material is soft and the walls are rounded and irregular, the quality of sound in an earthen building tends to be very pleasant. It is not dead and dry like in houses with wall-to-wall carpeting, and it is not hollow or cold, like in buildings with too much glass, steel and concrete. The earthen walls help bring our voices to life, make music sound beautiful and make "house sounds" (chopping food in the kitchen, closing doors, ticking clocks) a pleasant part of the whole living experience.

2.3 Light straw-clay

Visit www.HouseAlive.org *for pictures and videos on this chapter.*

With light straw-clay we coat straw with clay slip and then tamp it into the space between wooden studs or posts. It provides much more insulation than an earthen wall. Because there are so many poorly performing stud-frame houses in existence, it can make a great material for transforming a conventional house into a natural house. The clay coating on the straw makes it more fire and rodent resistant. The material can also be used (un-tamped) as attic insulation and in a somewhat wetter form as insulation for earthen ovens.

The load-bearing skeleton structure of the wall, around which the light straw-clay is tamped, can be made out of timbers, poles, dimensional lumber, brick or pillars of any kind (even cob). The wall should be at least three inches thick, otherwise the infill will be too thin and weak. The wall should not be too thick either as the material dries slowly; in all but the driest climates, anything wider than ten inches has a greater chance of developing mold inside the wall. For all but the coldest climates, a six or eight inch wall constructed in the warmer months will dry sufficiently and will perform well.

Ideally, the span between the load-bearing supports is between 12 and 24 inches. Anything wider than 24 inches can cause weakness in the wall, and additional studs or posts may be necessary. Framing additional 2 x 4's with the long end parallel to the wall (flat framing) can be really helpful.

Wires and water lines can be installed by drilling holes through the middle of the studs or posts and leading the pipes and wires through them. Outlet boxes can be nailed to the supports.

Making the mix

- Loosen a flake of straw in a wheelbarrow or on top of a tarp on the ground.
- Add a half-bucket of clay slip and mix it with the straw by hand until all of the straw is evenly coated.
- Use it right away. The straw quickly soaks up the moisture, drying the material out and less sticky if it sits for too long.

Tamping

- Use planks or plywood at least 10" wide to create a box form at the bottom of the framed wall. It's often convenient to work on a six or eight foot section of wall. You can use wood clamps or screws to temporarily attach the planks to the frame.
- Fill the form with the light straw-clay material and tamp it with a piece of wood, brick, or anything solid. Tamp about four inches at a time. Trying to do more may result in some sections not being fully compacted.
- As you add more light straw-clay, make sure that the top of the previous layer is somewhat "roughed-up" so that the layers can connect.
- Once you have reached the top of the form, loosen the clamps or screws and raise the planks so that the bottom of the planks overlap about the top two inches of the light straw-clay that you just tamped.
- Once you have reached the top of the wall, pack the last section with a shorter tamper and eventually just with your hands and fingers. If necessary, you can make the mix a little wetter to finish the top of the wall.

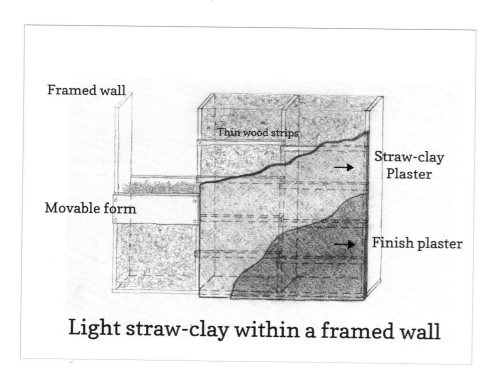

Light straw-clay within a framed wall

Finishing a light straw-clay wall

Depending on the span between the studs or posts, it is often advisable to nail some thin pieces of wood horizontally across the outside of the studs after you've filled the space with light straw-clay. This will give the wet light straw-clay some extra stability. Thin branches, strips of ¼" plywood, or something similar can be used for this purpose. Be careful to keep this reinforcement thin; otherwise, the following layer of straw-clay plaster needs to be very thick to cover the strips. Nailing some of these wood strips diagonally can also help make the framed wall stronger by creating cross bracing.

In barns, garages, outbuildings, and even in some sections of a house, it's possible to simply finish the wall by painting one or more coats of clay-slip over it. The wall will continue to look pretty rough, and will dust a little as well, but the straw will be protected from slowly degrading.

Allow the wall to fully dry before plastering it. Test it by reaching a finger into the middle of the wall; you shouldn't feel any moisture. Finish it by smearing a thick coat (between ½" and 2") of straw-clay plaster on both sides. After the straw-clay plaster is dry, you can finish the wall with an earthen plaster.

If a wooden stud/post is wider than three inches, it is a good idea to staple some burlap on the wood and overlap the light straw-clay by 2 inches or so. Attach the burlap to the light straw-clay with some 3 inch "staples" made through bending some wire. This "bridging" will make it so that any movement of the wood will not cause cracks in the finish plaster.

This may be helpful…

Renovating your house with earth

The natural building movement aims to change the paradigm of how homes are currently built, from expensive, toxic, resource-intensive boxes, to elegant, affordable, healthy homes that make sense for the planet and us. The pioneers in this field have already created many beautiful homes that are different and give us hope for a better world. The question remains: What are we going to do with the other 100,000,000 homes in the USA that have the potential to last another 50+years?

Buildings seldom fail structurally. What fails is the stuff that we put on the inside and outside of them. Within 5 years a newly built home starts falling apart. The cause of this is the poor quality of the material and craftsmanship: kitchens built out of particleboard, bathrooms of cheap fiberglass, walls out of drywall, siding out of compressed sawdust or plastic, roofs out of tar and flooring out of synthetic carpet. All these materials look somewhat OK when they are new but they don't age gracefully. Altogether they are not materials you want to be close to. The components with a much longer lifespan are the framing, the foundation, the electrical and plumbing and the roof structure. However, when too many parts of a building start to fail, in our economic system it becomes cheaper to tear down the building instead of fixing it up.

Other reasons why we'd rather do away with a building is because it is poorly designed and uncomfortable to be in. It feels too cold or too hot, has high utility bills and a floor plan that fits no one's needs. In other situations, property investors often tear down (sometimes perfectly good) small houses to build bigger ones that will provide more return on their investment.

The concept of "natural renovation" offers the possibility of remodeling existing houses with natural materials. The next time the drywall looks dented and disgusting, let's not replace it with drywall. When the tar roof starts to fall apart, let's not just tack another layer of tar upon it. And when the carpet gets stained and ugly and goes to the dump, let's see if we can find an alternative. We can make more pleasant spaces that people will want to live in and preserve by using simple earthen building techniques. Here are a few ideas:

Strip the building down to the foundation, floor and ceiling/roof structure. (If necessary, install some bracing to make sure the building stays straight without the siding and drywall). Then fill in the walls with light straw-clay and finish it with a straw-clay plaster and an earthen plaster. Install an earthen floor on top of the plywood subfloor. No more hollow walls for animals, no more mold, no more toxic paints.

If you would like to keep sections of drywall, plaster them, first with an inch or so of straw-clay plaster, and then with an earthen finish plaster. Make sure you rough up the drywall first so that the clay has something to grab on to.

Use cob or straw-clay plaster to round corners and sharp edges, giving the house a less industrial and assembled look. Finish it with an earthen plaster.

Use a clay paint to very inexpensively give a bedroom, kitchen or living room a soft earthen feel. Off course you can also do an earthen plaster directly on drywall. When doing the latter, first treat the drywall with a mixture of flour paste and sand, in order to give the surface some "teeth".

Use cob "pony walls" to divide oversized rooms into a few cozy spaces. These sculptural walls can be as thin as 3 inches, or, if your floor can support it, make them 18 inches thick and create extra shelving and cubbies inside the wall.

Bring definition to the outdoor spaces around your house with the addition of earthen garden walls. This will help make the spaces around your house attractive, intimate, and usable.

All these ideas can help you renovate your house in a very inexpensive and beautiful way!

2.4 Straw-clay plaster

Straw-clay plaster has two specific characteristics:
1. It has a high clay content, which makes it very sticky.
2. It contains a lot of chopped straw, which gives it a lot of strength.

Even though there is a lot of clay in this mix, this plaster is still very strong due to the enormous amount of short pieces of straw and therefore unlikely to crack. The clay still shrinks but cannot pull the material apart. Instead, the shrinking of the clay often leads to endless amounts of hardly visible hairline cracks. For some highly aggressive clays (the clay expands and shrinks a lot), large structural cracks could potentially form. In this case it can help to add some sand to the mix, or, if it happened just in a few places, you can fill those in later, again with the same material.

How to mix

It is easiest to mix straw-clay plaster in a wheelbarrow. Start by pouring two buckets of clay slip into the wheelbarrow, and continue by adding handfuls of chopped straw. The straw will soak up a lot of moisture. Mix with a hoe and keep adding straw until it becomes difficult to add any more. It always takes more than you think!

You can also mix it on a tarp, as is described in the cob section. Start with hydrated clay-soil and keep adding water and chopped straw. If the material starts spilling off the tarp, you have added too much water. You can fix that by adding more straw and/or dry clay-soil.

Applications

Because of its stickiness and strength, straw-clay plaster can be used in many aspects of earthen construction. It has often been called the "fix-all" of natural building. Below are some of the most common uses:

One-coat plaster
With the right mixture you can trowel this material on any surface and create a one-coat plaster. In other words, it won't need a finish coat. To achieve this the mix needs a lot of straw and the clay slip needs to be free of rocks and chunks. The end result can look like a smooth straw mat applied to the wall. This works well as an exterior finish, when it is not necessary to have a very smooth surface. As a contrast to a smooth earthen plaster, a straw-clay plaster can have a nice rustic effect.

Ceilings
You can create an earthen ceiling by stretching chicken wire, or some other wire mesh, between the ceiling rafters. You may choose to build it so that the rafters are visible by attaching the wire to the top of the rafters, or to the underside of the rafters so that the rafters are hidden.

- Start by stretching chicken wire over ceiling rafters, attaching it with staples to the top (or bottom) of the rafters. It is important to stretch the chicken wire very tightly between the rafters; the weight of the wet straw-clay plaster will make it sag a little, called "pillowing". A little of this can be attractive but too much pillowing can make the ceiling look "gloomy." Alternatives to using chicken wire can be willow branches staples about ½" apart, ½" hardware cloth, or rabbit fencing. These three options will help you create a ceiling that will "pillow" less, or not at all, depending on the span between the rafters.
- Smear about one inch layer of straw-clay plaster on top of the mesh, letting it squeeze through the holes in the chicken wire. While it is still wet, smooth the underside with a trowel. If you can't access the top of the ceiling, you can also apply the straw-clay plaster from the underside, pushing the material carefully up through the wire mesh. This is more time consuming.
- Once this layer has dried, finish the underside (the visible side) with an earthen plaster. Because plastering a ceiling can be cumbersome, to get the nicest results it sometimes is better to first apply another brown coat and make that layer very smooth and even. Also, experiment carefully with your finish coat, making it as sticky as you can without it cracking. This will help you in "fighting gravity" while plastering.

Three dimensional art

You can apply a straw-clay plaster to any surface, such as cob, plywood, drywall, even glass. This can give the wall an artistic touch or a whimsical character. When applying it to panes of glass, you can reshape a window opening, for example, creating the illusion of an arch.

Making blocks

Using straw-clay plaster to make building blocks will create strong blocks with a relatively high insulation value because of the high straw content. Make the mix dry enough so that when you lift up the form the material will keep its shape.

Brown coat

A brown coat prepares a wall for an earthen finish plaster. Often this can be done with a clay and sand mixture, essentially really wet cob without the straw. This works well because it can cover up little pieces of straw sticking out of the wall. However, a straw-clay plaster brown coat tends to be stronger, insulates the wall better, sticks to the wall easier (very useful for earthbag walls), and can be easier to smooth out.

If a building has thick walls, you can use a combination of hardware cloth and straw-clay plaster to shape the areas around windows and doors. The sill and sides can often be shaped by using cob (if you need to fill in a lot of space) or straw-clay plaster. Above windows and doors, hardware cloth can be stapled in a convex or concave shape and then coated with straw-clay plaster. It's usually a good idea to fill the cavity you create behind the hardware cloth with dry straw or some other form of insulation. On wood, attach the hardware cloth with staples; on cob, long screws with a big washer work well.

Transforming drywall with earth

Straw-clay plaster can be used to round corners and hard edges in a house, making it feel less like a manufactured house. You can also apply an inch or so on the drywall of an entire room or house. It will make the walls feel alive and more friendly to humans. It will also add a good amount of mass to the room, soften its acoustics, and moderate its humidity. If you are planning on covering drywall with straw-clay plaster, it is a good idea to first rough up the drywall, so that the plaster has something to cling to. This can be done with large screwdrivers, crow bars, claw hammers, and the like. Make sure you have a good scratch in the paper of the drywall about every 4 inches or so. Another possibility is to attach a lot of staples, nails or screws to create "teeth" for the plaster to adhere to. This can be more practical if the wall you are working on is made out of some form of wood.

Wattle and daub

Thin, non-loadbearing walls for interior partitions (or even entire buildings) can be made by weaving a matrix of flexible branches,like willow, between load bearing posts or studs, and then covering this with a straw-clay plaster. The holes in the weaving can be as large as 2 inches. Many of the stereotypical mud huts that we associate with the African continent are built this way. These structures do well in arid areas because rain is sporadic enough that any damage to the building can easily be repaired. The clay helps keep the interior relatively cool.

2.5 Building with blocks

Visit <u>www.HouseAlive.org</u> *for pictures and videos on this chapter.*

Building with blocks is similar to building with cob, with one major difference: the wall is constructed using dried blocks rather than wet cob. This comes with both advantages and disadvantages.

<u>Advantages</u>
- Blocks can be made ahead of time, making the actual raising of the walls faster. You can make a few blocks per week over a year's time, or make all the blocks in short amount of time with a large group of people.
- Getting the right mix is less critical than with cob. If a block cracks or is weak, you don't use it. You can also make the mix a little wetter than with cob, which makes the mixing process easier.
- It's easier to make the wall plumb and there is no need for trimming.

<u>Disadvantages</u>
- It is harder to do sculptural work with blocks. (Note: You can combine cob with block building in places where you want more sculptural details.)
- Block buildings are typically more "rectilinear" and have less of a hand-built feeling to them.
- The blocks are usually very heavy, and significant strength is needed to get them on top of the wall. A 4" x 12" x 16" block weighs about 35 pounds.
- Because there are seams between the blocks, block buildings are not as strong as cob buildings, which are essentially monolithic. This may be important in earthquake prone areas.
- You will need reliable dry weather and/or a large covered area for drying the blocks.

The Mix

For most block building, the mix of material is similar to cob. It can be a little wetter than cob as you don't have to build with it right away; as long as it holds its form while it is drying. There is more flexibility in the sand to clay ratio with block building because you are only drying one block, as opposed to a whole building. Too much clay can still cause the blocks to crack during the drying process, but you can just add some more sand to the mix. The clay-soil, sand, and straw are best mixed on a tarp the same way as with cob.

If it seems like the straw is very stiff, chop the straw. Otherwise, pieces of straw may stick out of the dried blocks, which may not be practical or desirable if you are planning to leave the bricks exposed. Generally, the more straw you put in the mix, the stronger the blocks will be. However, at some point too much straw will turn the blocks into light straw-clay blocks, with the clay-soil holding the straw together rather than the straw providing tensile strength for the clay-soil/sand mix. Blocks with more straw will become lighter, provide more insulation, and will at some point, once it has too much straw in it, not be load-bearing anymore.

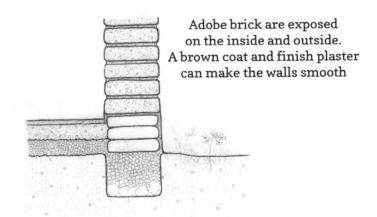

Adobe brick are exposed on the inside and outside. A brown coat and finish plaster can make the walls smooth

Adobe brick wall system

Forms

Make a form out of dimensional lumber. Long screws and/or metal or plywood reinforcements in the corners will help keep the form square. Obviously, the dimensions of the inside of the form will determine the size of the blocks. If you make the blocks too thin (less than three inches) there is a greater chance they will break. If they are too thick and large, they can be too heavy to handle. If you leave the blocks exposed, think about the visual effect you create. Aim for a pleasing proportionality between the thickness and length of the block and the layers of mortar between them. Also, smaller buildings will look better if built with smaller blocks.

Making blocks

Wet the inside of the form with water and set it on a flat area. It's helpful if the ground under the form is sandy so that the brick can be easily lifted up once it's dried. Fill the form with the cob mix and shape the top with a trowel or straight piece of wood. The top and bottom of the block will never be visible so it doesn't need to be perfectly smooth. Now carefully lift up the form, leaving the wet block in place. When you make your next block, ensure that the blocks are about six inches apart.

You may find that the material will stick to the wood form. Make sure the wood is smooth, perhaps oiled; lining the wood with sheet metal can help. A slight tapping on the sides of the form can also help loosen the mix from the form. Keep the form wet and clean as you work.

Drying

After a day or two of good drying weather your blocks will be dry enough to carefully lift up on one side to stand on edge. This will expose more surface area to air and will speed up the drying process; it will take anywhere from a few days to a few weeks for your blocks to fully dry, depending on the weather. Although the bricks can usually handle a light rain, it's better to cover them if it rains. In areas where it rains often, form the blocks under a shelter or cover them after they have been formed. Whatever cover you use, make sure that it has air circulation around the blocks, otherwise they won't dry well. Make your blocks as close to the building site as possible so you won't need to move them far.

Construction

Building with blocks is pretty straightforward, and many of us have had lots of practice as kids. Here are a few pointers:
- Always avoid vertical seams and start with whole blocks on corners and near windows, doors, and other potentially weak spots. 1/2 blocks should go in the middle of a wall.
- For rectilinear buildings use a horizontal string line as a guide for the next layer of blocks, helping you keep the wall plumb, level and straight. Use a line-level.
- You can curve a wall with blocks, however you will need a 4-foot level to check for plumb while you are building. For strong curves you can make special blocks that are shorter on one side (trapezoidal).
- The mortar between the blocks is made from the same material as the blocks but without the straw.
- If you plan to leave the blocks exposed, avoid bringing the mortar all the way to the edge of the block. Rather, fill the last bit in later with a tool the width of the joint and give it a nice, smooth finish. Having the joint set in a little will make the blocks and the wall look better.

- Putting a brown coat/straw-clay plaster and finish earthen plaster over the blocks will protect them better from rain and wind erosion on the outside and will make for smooth, dust free walls inside.

Connections

For doors, windows, and cabinets, pieces of wood need to be installed in the walls to provide places to attach fasteners. You can build a wooden frame that's the same size as a block and place it in the wall as you're building. The leftover space can be filled with fresh cob. (This is sometimes called a "Gringo block.")

The most secure way to attach a roof is to make the last foot of your wall out of very strong cob and embed dead-men into that layer. You can increase the strength of this top layer by placing layers of long sticks or bamboo horizontally in the middle of the cob, making it function more like a bond-beam.

This may be helpful…

How earthen buildings last

Some of the oldest buildings and structures on the planet are made out of earth. Parts of the Great Wall of China were made out of adobe brick, as were some of the pyramids in Egypt. Devon county in England is known for having entire towns, hundreds of years old, built out of cob. And in the United States, New Mexico, we find the Taos Pueblo, a cluster of multi-storied buildings that have been continuously inhabited for over 1,000 years. It was probably built between 1000 and 1450 A.D., and as of 2006 it has 150 inhabitants.

Generally speaking, if you want your earthen house to last a very long time, anywhere between 100 and 1000 years, the most important thing to consider in your building process is a solid foundation and a good roof. A good foundation makes sure that the building does not settle unevenly due to its weight and protects the earthen walls from possible flooding and ground moisture. A roof with plenty of overhang will protect the walls from getting soaked and softened in the rain. This is not to suggest that earthen walls disintegrate easily; in many arid climates, people leave earthen buildings exposed to the rain and just fix up the wear and tear every now and then.

In this context, it is important to stress another factor, sometimes even more important than a foundation and a roof, that determines the longevity of a building: a loving relationship between the building and the people who use it. Earthen buildings tend to be more "lovable" for many reasons: they were made out of earth rather than industrially produced materials; they were built by hand, often with help of the greater community; they provide great comfort and beauty; repairs are simple and inexpensive; and they have a possibility of relieving people of the questionable practices of housing speculation and mortgages. The average house in the United States has a life expectancy of less than 50 years. And often it gets demolished, not because the house/roof/foundation is failing, but rather because the house was never really loved. Tired looking drywall and once fashionable looking building materials become too expensive to replace and housing speculation makes it worthwhile to tear the building down and ship it off to the dump. How sad for the people who built it and lived in it, as well as for our environment.

I believe it is reasonable to consider that houses last longer not necessarily due to the strength of the building materials, but rather because of the quality of the material. Buildings made out of glass, steel and concrete are much stronger than earthen buildings. However, a little damage looks really bad right away and is expensive to repair. We also physically and emotionally resist the hard, cold and industrial qualities of these materials.

Should it be our goal to make buildings last as long as possible? Perhaps, in the interest of stability, security, creating a home and community, such a strategy would be advised. However, a simple earthen cabin, built with joy and then used for a little while can just as easily melt back into the earth without much of a financial or environmental cost. Looking at it from this angle, earth is also the material you want to use for when you just want to create beautiful, temporary shelter. From 10 years to 1000 years, earth is the building material of choice and will do the job just right!

2.6 Earthbag Construction

Visit www.HouseAlive.org *for pictures and videos on this chapter.*

Earthbag construction is essentially a form of building with blocks. Rather than forming and drying the blocks first, you form them on the wall as it is built. Polypropylene bags are the form in which the earthen material dries. Different size bags can be used to achieve different wall widths. Burlap or coffee sacks are not recommended for any but the most temporary of projects.

Different mixes

Because the bags stay with the building, there is some freedom in terms of their content; as the bags last, so will the wall. The theory is that the poly material can last for hundreds of years as long as it is covered with plaster or kept away from sunlight any other way. Three different fill materials that can be used for earthbag construction are described below.

- Any sandy, silty, or rocky material can be used. The bags will hold the material together. This works well for garden walls, flood banks, emergency shelters, and temporary structures.
- Moist clay-soil can be used for structural walls in houses. Because the bags are very porous, the clay-soil will dry out and the filled bags essentially become adobe bricks.
- Cement stabilized material, such as clay-soil or some combination of clay-soil, sand, and/or rocks mixed with cement can be used, creating a version of concrete block. This is useful for stem walls for foundation systems: the cement will stabilize the material so it won't get soft when wet. Even though the bags should hold the blocks together if they get wet, the addition of cement to the mix is extra insurance for structures you hope will last a long time.

Mixing the material

If there is no clay-soil or cement in your mix, you can fill the bags without any mixing. If you use only clay-soil and it is already moist, you can also fill the bags without mixing. Often you will need to moisten the mix a little so the cement and/or the clay can be activated and become the glue for the mix. Here are the steps:

- Put two buckets of material in a wheelbarrow. If you plan to add cement, do so after you have added the first bucket. Add one shovelful of cement for each bucket of material. Add more cement, sand, and rocks if you want to get closer to a real concrete mix. (Concrete is one part cement, two parts sand, and three parts gravel/rocks.)

- Add a little water.
- Mix with a hoe. It's easiest to mix with another person, switching sides often to ensure you get every corner of the wheelbarrow.
- Check the mix. Grab a handful, squeeze it hard, and see if it sticks together, like a dry snowball or moist gardening soil. This is the same consistency as would be used for rammed earth and rammed tire walls. If you make it any wetter, the tamping will not work because it will turn the bag into a wet blob.

Filling the bags

It's best to fill the bags directly on the wall where you are building, or as close as possible so you don't have to carry them far. If you do have to transport them, a dolly/hand-truck is really handy. To help keep the bags open while filling them, you can use an old bucket with the bottom cut out of it. Place the bucket upside down (so the widest part is on the bottom) and wrap the top of the bag over the edge. This makes it easier to get a shovelful of fill material in the bag. Before filling bags, turn them inside out. This will prevent the corners from sticking out like ears and will make it easier to plaster the wall or foundation.

Tamping the bags

Once a bag is about three quarters full of material, set it on the wall and proceed as follows:

- Roll the top of the bag closed, about three rotations. If you can't do that, you have filled the bag up with too much material.
- Carefully lay the bag flat, ensuring that the rolled-up part is snug against the end of the previous bag. This way the top cannot unroll and the material will stay in the bag. If you are starting a new row or have nothing to butt up against, use two bags and place the rolled-up parts of them against each other.
- Stand on the bag and gently tap it with your feet, giving the bag roughly the right shape. Evaluate its position, estimating how much it will expand once tamped, and adjust it a bit with your hands as necessary.
- Use an 8x8 inch metal plate tamper to tamp the bag. As the bag is tamped, it will grow in surface area and the sound of the tamping will change. Tamp enough to get to a nice solid "wap." Don't over-tamp or tamp with too much force; the top of the bag will start to unroll or the fabric may tear if you do so.
- With a two-pound hammer or a block of wood, make a small indentation, with a surface area of about 2" x 4" inches and a depth of 1 inch, on top of and in between the two most recently tamped bags. The bag that is placed on the next layer will sink into this indentation while being tamped, helping to connect the layers.

Avoid walking on the bags or moving them around during the drying process, especially if you have cement in them.

An 8x8 plate tamper

Other considerations

- For rounded walls fill a bag a little less than usual and then move the material with your hands so that when you roll the top, you have an angle in the bag. This feels a bit clumsy when you do it for the first time, but it really works.
- Once a row is almost done, fill the last bag with just enough material to fill in the gap and roll it up with extra rotations as necessary. Avoid putting half-filled bags on corners or near other weak spots such as windows.
- Whenever possible, lay your bags the way you would bricks, avoiding continuous vertical seams. This is called a "running bond." This sometimes means adding a half-filled bag to the row just to avoid the vertical seams.

- Wires and water pipes can be installed between rows, as in cob. Use sleeves for water pipes that go through the wall, as described in the chapter on cob.
- When building structural walls or high garden walls, use a level to make sure your walls are plumb.
- For foundations, it's nice to start with a layer of large rocks or broken pieces of concrete (urbanite). This will keep the bags off the ground, preventing any moisture from wicking into them. Because the bags will take the shape of whatever is underneath them, you don't have to be an expert stone builder to get that first layer in place; as long as the various stones don't differ in level more than 2 inches.

Finishing bags

It is important to plaster the bags as soon as you can, in order to protect them from UV light. If you don't have time to do so right away, paint them with clay slip to keep off most of the sunlight. After that do the following:

Fill in the seams between the bags with a straw-clay plaster or with a cob mix that has a high clay contents, so it sticks well to the bags. Fill the seams so they become flush with the outside of the bags.

Cover the bags with a straw-clay plaster, finding connection points with the mix between the seams.

Finish with an earthen finish plaster as you like.

For bag foundations in very wet climates, one option is to staple chicken wire to the bags and then use cement stucco to protect the bags. You can avoid using cement by stacking rocks up against the foundation after you have finished the bags with a straw-clay plaster. This will keep any driving rain from eroding the earthen materials and can also create a beautiful effect.

this may be helpful…

How heavy buildings work

Earthen buildings tend to be heavy or "massive" (lots of mass). Using this mass in the right way can lead to a house that is much more comfortable than conventional, lightweight houses. The heavier a house is, the more heat it can store. The walls of an earthen house are like a giant thermal "battery," that can be "charged" by heat from inside the house, like a wood stove or heating system, or by heat from outside the house, namely the sun.

Massive walls do take a long time to heat up. If you were to start with cold walls, it could take a few days of running your heat source (wood stove or furnace) before the walls are fully "charged." Once that has happened, only a normal amount of heat input will be required to maintain a comfortable interior temperature. And just as it took a long time to warm up the house, it will take a long time for it to cool off. In an earthen house, you can often turn the heat off in the evening and wake up the next morning to a comfortable temperature.

Heavy buildings work best when there is plenty of sunlight in the winter, to help with the heating of the house. Solar energy will help "charge" the walls by shining in through well placed south-facing windows, generating a lot of heat inside the house, as well as warming up the walls on the outside. Thus, in climates that require a heat source, earthen buildings should be carefully located, so as to take full advantage of the free energy that can be obtained from the sun. The end result is an efficient house with a pleasant and stable indoor temperature.

In the summer, when we want to keep the house cool, the mass of earthen walls can help absorb excess heat. Again, the walls get "charged." At night we can open windows to allow cooler air to circulate through the house and carry away the heat that was stored in the walls. This again results in a house with a temperature that doesn't fluctuate that much. The greater the temperature difference between night and day, and the more the air circulates, the better this process works.

Lots of mass is also nice during extreme weather events, such as heat waves and cold snaps. If the walls are thick and heavy enough, the storage capacity can significantly moderate the uncomfortable temperature fluctuations that are often associated with such events, without air conditioners or electric room heaters.

In some climates, there can even be a seasonal effect: it takes many months to fully warm up the walls in the summer, which then carries over to at least part of the colder season. This works if you live in a sunny climate, with hot summers and cold winters and have really thick earthen walls.

Mass in a house does not have to be just in the outside walls. It can be in the floor in the form of an earthen or clay-tile floor (concrete floors are heavy but not pleasant to live on), it can be in the form of internal walls made out of heavy materials, or even heavy things you bring into the house. Water has a great ability to store heat. Filling a large steel drum with water and placing it in front of a sunny window can provide a lot of stored heat for the winter (and be a heat sink in the summer too) This trick can be used as a simple house modification that can lead to lower energy bills and greater comfort (make sure your floor can handle the weight!).

Is there such a thing as too much mass in a building? Perhaps in extremely cold climates with very little sun, it's better to have exterior walls that are highly insulative. Mass on the inside will still help with temperature fluctuations and storing heat. Also, houses in cold climates that are only used intermittently, such as mountain cabins, may be better off with having not too much mass; if you are only there for a short time, you don't want to spend the first two days heating up the walls! Other than that, most people in most climates will benefit from bringing more mass into their house.

2.7 Earthen finish plasters

Visit <u>www.HouseAlive.org</u> *for pictures and videos on this chapter.*

An earthen finish plaster is a finish coat that can be applied to earthen walls, usually over a brown coat of straw-clay plaster or sand-clay plaster. It can also go directly on drywall, plywood, OSB, and concrete block walls. It is usually between ¼" and ⅛" inch thick and made out of finely screened materials. It can be used on both the inside and outside of buildings. You may prefer the outside walls of buildings to just have a nicely troweled brown coat rather than a fine earthen finish plaster.

Making the plaster

An earthen finish plaster is made out of three basic materials:
- Sand: The grains need to be angular to provide structure to the plaster and small to make the surface very smooth. If you want a light colored plaster, you need light colored sand. You can buy "Monterey beach sand," grit #60, for its light color. Other sands are also a possibility, such as quarts sand. For darker colors screening any sand through a window screen will do.
- Clay: This needs to be free of chunks and rocks. For light plasters or if you want to add pigments to the plaster use a white potter's clay, such as kaolin clay. For darker colors most screened clay-soils will be fine. Depending on the type of clay, it may improve workability to soak a pre-measured amount of dry clay prior to mixing the plaster. The longer clay soaks, the more hydrated it becomes and the easier it is to use.
- Flour paste: The gluten in the flour helps make the plaster stronger and dust free. To make flour paste, boil four quarts of water in a large pot. Mix one quart (four cups) of white flour with a whisk into two quarts of cold water. Once the large pot boils, add the cold mix to the boiling water and stir over a low flame until it becomes the consistency of gravy.

The plaster mix needs to have enough clay to stick to the wall and enough sand so it won't crack when it dries. It's easiest to mix the plaster in a five gallon bucket using a drill with a paint paddle attachment. Mixing plaster in a wheelbarrow using a hoe also works. Whatever you mix it in, always make sure that the container and tools are clean.

Making several small test batches beforehand to check for strength and cracking is essential. A basic starter mix is two parts dry clay (perhaps soaked in advance), one part flour paste, and four parts sand. You want a plaster mix that feels silky and is still on the cusp of being liquid. Because the flour paste is an organic material, you should not mix up more plaster than you can reasonably use in one or two days. Check to make sure your tests do not have any cracks in them; if cracks appear try adding more sand to the mix.

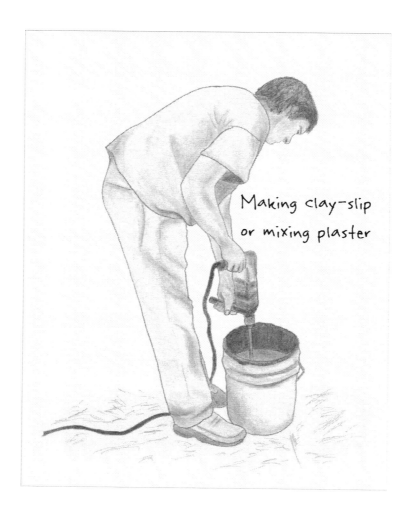

Making clay-slip or mixing plaster

Cracks can also happen where two different building materials meet in a wall, such as where a cob wall meets a wooden post. To reduce this kind of cracking, bridge the seam with a piece of burlap, stapled to the wood and attached with a little clay slip to the cob surface. Then plaster over the burlap with straw-clay plaster. Another cause of cracking could be when the plaster dries too quickly (plastering in the hot sun) or dries unevenly due to varying thickness in the finish coat.

When working with any fine powders such as powdered clay or quarts sand, always wear a dust mask or bandana around your nose and mouth and avoid standing downwind from the dust.

112

Other plaster additives

Adding iron oxide powders to the plaster mix is an easy way to get a variety of colors. They are non-toxic and inexpensive and can be purchased from pottery or concrete supply stores, as well as online. The colors are usually soft and earthy, such as mustard yellow to orange, red, and brown. Pre-mix the color with water before you add it to the plaster. Often one cup of iron oxide per bucket of plaster will add enough color to the mix, but this varies, depending on the color of your clay and sand. Experiment and test!

Clay can be found in many different colors, such as white, yellow, pink, orange, red, blue, purple, brown, grey, black, and more. Look for interesting colors of clay in road cuts and other locations, they can make spectacular plasters.

Finely chopped and screened straw (or any other fibers) can add strength to the mix as well as give an interesting visual effect. Make sure the fibers are short and flexible, and preferably sifted through a window screen.

One third of your clay can be replaced by cow manure to make the plaster stronger. When fresh, the manure contains enzymes that increase the strength of the plaster and make it more water resistant. It is best to hydrate the clay/manure mix and let it ferment for a few days before using it as a plaster. Horse manure can be added as a fiber source. Let the horse manure dry and then grate it on a screen.

Preparing the surface

It's important that the brown coat is as smooth as possible. An earthen plaster can usually correct scratches and indentations in the brown coat up to ¼" deep. Use masking tape where you want to create a crisp line (when changing colors or plastering around sculptural features, for example). Cover the floor and any other surfaces that you do not want to get dirty.

Applying the plaster

The following method is foolproof for novice plasterers:

- With a large wet sponge or spray bottle, dampen a section of the wall, between one and two square yards. The wall should change color, but don't make it so wet that water runs down the wall.
- With a plastering tool or your hands, smear the plaster on the wall in ping-pong ball sized amounts, and spread it flat until it's about 1/4 inch thick at the most.
- With a pool trowel, Japanese trowel, or a yogurt container lid with the rim cut off, smooth the plaster out as well as you can. Don't worry too much about trowel marks.

- Start the next section of wall. Start at the very top of the wall and work down; otherwise, you will damage your work.
- Allow the plaster to dry somewhat, but not entirely. You want it so that it is still soft but has set up. We call this being "leather hard", because it feels almost like leather. How quickly it reaches this point will depend on the temperature, humidity, and air movement in the room. It can take anywhere from 10 minutes to an hour. Once it reaches this point, take a moist sponge and smooth out the plaster by lightly rubbing the wall in a circular motion. All the roughness and marks will be smoothed out, and you can easily blend the various sections together seamlessly as long as they are not completely dry.

You now have two choices as to how to finish the plaster:

1. You can use a yogurt container lid and burnish the wall in a circular motion, as if waxing a car. By pressing hard, you can push in the grains of sand that are sitting

on the surface of the plaster. The more you do this, the harder and more durable your plaster will be. Again, the plaster has to be leather dry in order for this to work.

2. If you don't want to burnish your plaster, wait until it is dry (the color will get lighter). Then take a hard brush and sweep off any grains of sand that are sitting on the surface of the plaster.

If it still seems like your wall is dusty, you can paint a layer of flour paste over it. This goes on very easily with a paint roller or brush and dries completely clear. This works amazingly well!

More experienced plasterers can often bypass the sponging and burnishing stage, depending on the plaster mix, the tools they use, and the smoothness of the subsurface. Feel free to experiment. Plastering is a skill that may take some time to develop. The above method works well for most people.

This may be helpful...

Protecting an earthen house from moisture

Earthen building techniques, as described here, use un-stabilized earth as a primary building material. The material becomes hard and strong because it dries out, not because of some irreversible chemical reaction, as is the case with concrete. This makes earthen buildings easy to repair, totally natural and fully recyclable. However, people unfamiliar with earthen building often express the fear that the first rainstorm will cause a structure to melt back to the ground. Yet in reality, some of the oldest buildings in the world are made out of un-stabilized earth. So how is this possible?

In wet climates, the best way to to protect an earthen building is with "a good hat and a good pair of boots." The hat refers to the roof, which must be leak-free and have a good overhang to keep rain off the walls; the "boots" is the foundation that keeps the earth at least a foot or so off the ground. In extreme dry climates, where there is usually little wood available for roof construction, roofs made out of earth are not unheard of. After a rare rainstorm, people go back onto the roof to fix whatever damage may have occurred. This type of roof is not practical for most climates and people.

Even with a good overhang the walls may get wet, due to wind driven rain. In this situation the outer surface of the wall will absorb some of the moisture, and the clay in the plaster will swell a little, making it harder for additional water to soak into the wall. Under most circumstances, this mechanism alone can be enough to protect your walls from major wear and tear. I have lived with earthen walls in Southern Oregon now for more than 10 years and for the most part they still look identical to when they were first built.

If you get an occasional major storm with sideways rain, you may want to take a little time every couple of years to patch worn areas. This is very easy to do, won't cost you anything, and is certainly much more pleasant and less time consuming than painting. Just remove any loose material and add some fresh to it. This could be cob or some sort of earthen plaster.

As we consider areas with more regular wind driven rain, other protective measures can be considered. One idea is to protect the house (or at least the side that gets most affected) from the wind by strategically positioning shrubs, trees, or earth berms as a windbreak. This will have the added benefit that it will make your house quieter as well as warmer in the winter.

Another approach is to make earthen plasters more water resistant. Burnishing (polishing the plaster by rubbing it and making it smooth) will make it harder for water to cause damage. Adding a few tablespoons of linseed oil to a bucket of plaster will make it a little more water resistant.

Adding manure to a plaster can also improve its durability: 10-20% of the plaster mix can be made out of slightly fermented cow manure.

If even more water resistance is needed, simply painting a layer of linseed oil on the wall can do the trick. Note that this seals the wall, making it more difficult for any moisture inside of the wall to migrate to the outside of the wall. Under extreme circumstances (in tiny houses, or when there is lots of cooking and showering without venting) this could increase humidity inside and cause mold to grow. You may choose to do this only on the lower part of the wall.

Using lime, either as a paint or a plaster, is another way to add a moisture resistant barrier to an earthen wall. Lime is produced by burning limestone in a kiln at a high temperature and after some other processes turns into a white powder. This is then mixed with water in order to produce a "lime putty," which has the texture of soft wet clay. Once wet lime is exposed to air, it converts through a chemical reaction back to limestone again, hence its durability. Lime putty works better if it sits for a while before it is used (anywhere from a week to a year or more). Store it in a sealed container and covered with a couple inches of water (a "water seal"); if the putty dries out, it will convert back into limestone and will be unusable.

To make lime paint, mix some putty with more water until it takes on the consistency of paint, and then apply it on to the wall with a brush. This technique is sometimes referred to as a "white wash," and is commonly used worldwide. To make a lime plaster, mix 1 part putty with 2-3 parts of sand (add water as needed and make sure you do tests!). Plasters are applied thicker than paints, and are therefore more durable. Lime plasters are applied just as you would do with an earthen plaster.

Lime paints and plasters are very light in color (white and pastels), which in hot climates can help keep a building cool. I have seen entire villages in the mountains of southern Spain that are regularly whitewashed, which increases the thickness of the lime paint over the years. You can add pigments if you don't want the light color.

A lime plaster or paint will adhere well to earthen walls and allow moisture to travel through fairly well (not as well as earth, but much better than an oiled wall). Lime is not as fun and easy to work with as earthen plasters and paints; it's technically not much harder, but it sets faster (and irreversible) and is also more dangerous to work with. Always wear safety glasses and protect your skin from splash while mixing and working with lime; it's very caustic and can cause burns. Lime can be purchased in different forms. In the United States, the most common lime used for building projects is called "type S", which is available in most hardware and mason supply stores.

Many people ask if cement based plasters (Stucco) can be used on earthen walls. This should be avoided! Stucco does not adhere well to earthen walls, and also traps moisture inside. In colder climates, moisture traveling from the inside of the house to the outside will build up against the plaster and condense. This can cause mold and damage to the earthen wall, as well as crack the concrete when it freezes.

2.8 Earthen floors

Visit www.HouseAlive.org *for pictures and videos on this chapter.*

An earthen floor is the last, finished, ¾" of earth on top of a subfloor. It is stabilized with linseed oil so that heavy foot traffic and water won't damage the floor. Earthen floors can be put on a tamped subfloor or on more conventional subfloors such as plywood, OSB, or a concrete slab.

Making a tamped subfloor

In this case the grade (the earth) is built up to where you would like to have the finished floor on the ground level of your building. This layer is referred to as a tamped floor and consists of two layers separated by a vapor barrier.

The first layer is the drainage layer, consisting of rock or rubble that can easily drain water. Its primary function is to ensure that moisture from the earth does not wick up into the floor. The drainage layer can be made out of round river rock, or crushed rock. The rocks should be about 1" in diameter, and not contain finer grains that would clog up the spaces between the rocks. Crushed glass can also be used. The drainage layer should be between two and six inches thick, depending on the amount of moisture you expect under the most extreme, wet circumstances.

A vapor barrier should be placed on top of the drainage layer. This is a tarp or piece of plastic that provides additional protection from moisture moving up into the floor. It is possible to use several smaller pieces of plastic, as long as you allow for generous overlaps. It is easy to find scrap pieces of plastic from building sites and lumber yards.

This is also a good place to insulate the floor by creating a thermal break between the drainage layer and the tamped floor, making it harder for heat to transfer into the earth through conduction. You can layer several pieces of plastic or tarps with broken glass, pumice rock, or vermiculite between the layers.

On top of the vapor barrier is the final layer of the sub-floor, usually four to seven inches of a mixture of crushed rock, sand, and clay. You can often purchase this mixture from a material yard under the name "road base" (used to make hard gravel roads). You can also make it yourself by buying ¾" minus and mixing it with loose clay-soil (¾" minus is gravel of varying sizes, ¾" in diameter and smaller). In new construction tamped floors are best made right after the stem wall has been built and before the walls go up. Follow these steps for making a tamped floor:

- Put a two-inch layer of road base on the vapor barrier. If you are making your own road base, first put down the 3/4 inch minus and then rake in some dry, powder like clay-soil, about five buckets per 100 square feet. The clay-soil does not have to be screened.
- Moisten this layer lightly using a hose with a sprayer attachment. Add just enough water so that the material changes color, but not more. If it gets too wet, you can't tamp it anymore.
- Rake this layer to make sure all material is damp.
- Tamp this layer with an 8x8 metal plate tamper. Don't forget the edges. (Go around several times to double check this.) For larger buildings you can rent a gas-powered tamper (jumping jack or plate compactor), which can comfortably tamp four inches at a time. Be careful to stay a foot away from the stem wall with this machine as its force could damage it. Rather, tamp the area next to the foundation by hand.
- Repeat the previous step several times until you have reached the desired floor level, leaving ¾" for the finished floor. As you work your way up, pay attention to making the tamped floor level. The easiest way to do this is to put a level on a long, straight board. Mark the wall with a piece of chalk where you want the top of the tamped floor to be. Getting the tamped floor as level and smooth as possible will make installing the finished floor a breeze. If possible measure level from just one reference point to avoid multiplying mistakes.

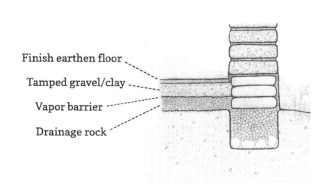

Finish earthen floor

Tamped gravel/clay

Vapor barrier

Drainage rock

Tamped floor with finish earth floor

The tamped floor will dry while you build the rest of the house. The finished floor will be the last thing you do before you move in.

Earthen floors on conventional subfloors

Finished earthen floors will just as easily go on top of conventional building materials such as plywood or concrete. Remember the following before installing an earthen floor on these surfaces:

- Whatever subsurface you use, it needs to be very stable. Wood floors with flexing floor joists need to be reinforced. Jump up and down forcefully in several spots to see if you detect significant movement of bounce. Plank floors will often move too much and can cause the earthen floor to crack. Covering them with ¼" plywood or OSB can remedy this. It's better if the subfloor is screwed in rather than nailed; screws are more stable, while nails can pop up out of the floor.
- With plywood or OSB floors, cover the seams between the sheets with duct tape. This prevents moisture from seeping into the seams and potentially damaging the plywood. With concrete slabs, fill any big cracks with a silicone-type substance.
- Any moisture problems with concrete slabs need to be resolved before the finished earthen floor is laid; there should be no transference of water vapor from the ground through the concrete. This could mean painting the concrete with a sealer or covering it with a plastic vapor barrier.
- For transitions into other rooms (or outside) where there is not an earthen floor, make sure there is a wooden, metal, or concrete sill that the floor can be poured against.
- Count on not being able to use the space for a two to four week period, depending on the drying time.

The finished floor

The finished floor is made out of three materials: angular screened sand, screened clay-soil, and finely chopped straw. The coarser the sand, the stronger your floor will be, but also the harder it will be to get a very smooth surface. Sand used for cement-stucco plaster works well; it is finer than concrete sand but less fine than finish plaster sand.

Because the floor doesn't have to fight gravity it can be very low in clay and high in sand. The straw in the mix makes for an interesting visual effect, gives the floor a little softness and insulation, and also provides some extra strength.

All ingredients can easily be mixed in a wheelbarrow using hoes. Mixing with two people and alternating sides of the wheelbarrow can ensure that all the material is mixed well.

Always do a test of about 3' x 3' feet to make sure that your recipe will work. A common mix to start with is one bucket of clay-soil (soaking dry clay-soil in advance can be helpful), three buckets of sand, and half a bucket of chopped straw. Mix the ingredients and add water as needed. You are looking for a consistency that is just barely liquid.

When you do a test, trowel some mix onto a flat surface, let it dry, and make sure it doesn't crack and that it turns into a hard, well-connected unit. Don't worry about dusting at this point; the linseed oil will greatly help in stabilizing the floor.

How to apply the final layer of a finished floor:
- On a tamped floor, slightly moisten the surface first, just enough so it changes color. Don't make it very wet, as these floors are slow to dry.
- Open windows for ventilation as necessary and plan your exit strategy; don't work yourself into a corner. Fans can greatly reduce the drying time. Hang them from the ceiling or put them in windowsills, making sure you can turn them on (from the outside) after the floor has been troweled.
- Empty one bucket of material at a time on the subfloor, spread it out with your hands and smooth with your trowel.
- Use a pool trowel to get an even layer. This is easier than you think. Estimate the ¾" thickness or use a little piece of 1 x 4 to guide you. You can make the floor as thin as ½" inch or as thick as 1 ½". Remember that thinner means less drying time. Thicker floors will add more thermal mass to the house. In houses with uneven subfloors, the earthen floor can compensate a little for that. If the subfloor is very uneven, more than ½", you may decide to pour a base coat first to create a more even surface for the finish layer.

- Turn on the fans and crank up the heat to facilitate drying. Floors that stay wet for longer than a week can start to mold and any seeds in mix (from the seed heads left in the straw) may sprout.

A few more pointers:
- To help prevent mold issues under poor drying circumstances, add a cup of borax to each wheelbarrow of mix.
- Floors don't need to be perfectly flat; they feel more comfortable and natural if they have some imperfections in them. However, try to get yours as smooth and even as possible; the imperfections will show up anyway!

Oiling the floor
Linseed oil is the best and most economical oil to use. Make sure you buy boiled linseed oil and not raw linseed oil. The floor should only be oiled once it has fully dried, usually indicated by a complete lightening of the color. For better penetration, warm up the oil a bit by putting the can in the sun or in pot of hot water for a few hours. Pour the warm oil on a small section of the floor and gently spread it with a brush or rag. Once you have done the whole floor, do at least two more coats. You don't need to wait in between coats or dilute subsequent coats. The second and third oilings will require a lot less oil than the first as the floor becomes more saturated.

Remember:

- Always make sure the area you oil is well ventilated.
- Make sure no oil sits on top of the floor; it needs to be absorbed by the floor or mopped up with a rag. Otherwise, you will end up with a sticky layer of linseed oil that can take forever to dry.
- Rags saturated with linseed oil can spontaneously combust, especially when left crumpled up. When you are done, dry them flat on a line or weighted down with stones, well away from combustible materials.
- The oil will dry in a matter of days. The linseed oil smell can linger for a month (or more), but becomes tolerable after a week or so.
- The floor will remain soft for a few weeks while the linseed oil is slowly setting up. Although you can use the floor during this time, it is better to use floor protecting "coasters" under tables, chairs and other heavy furniture to avoid making indentations.
- Oiled floors dry very dark, which makes them perfect for soaking up sunlight in passive solar houses. If you want some color in your floor, experiment with adding iron oxide pigments to either the floor mix or the oil mix. Both will work. Do some tests to see how much you need and what color you like.

Maintenance of earthen floors

- Sweeping and wet mopping can keep the floor clean and fresh looking.
- Linseed oil will disintegrate over time, as it is an organic product made from flax seed. Every two to five years, a fresh layer of oil will make your floor look new again.

- Sometimes a small piece of the floor gets damaged. To fix, it, first clean the edges of the damaged area and cut away any irregularities. A pocketknife works well for this. Make some floor mix, trowel it into the hole, let it dry, and oil it a few times. The seams will remain visible, adding character to your floor.

This may be helpful…

Earthen buildings and the building code

We get many questions about how earthen construction works in conjunction with the building code. Here are some of our insights:

1. Building regulation is necessary
Buildings influence more than just your own life. They should be built to high standards of health and safety and consider the surrounding area and resource management. If your house catches on fire, your neighbor's house might too, and so might the forest around you.

Unfortunately, building codes have morphed into a narrow set of safety regulations, mostly geared toward using commercial building products and meeting engineering standards. In some ways this has been a success story, in particular for the finances of the building product industry, banks, tax collectors, realtors, architects, insurance companies, contractors, and housing developers. Additionally, the larger buildings in our ever-growing cities require good oversight to ensure they are safe. High-rises, football stadiums and apartment complexes should have high engineering standards!

For those of us who want to pursue a more simple life, building codes seem like an obstacle. The codes seem to push the building industry toward structures that are more complex, more expensive, more toxic, and with more square feet. It would be nice if there was one standard for large, complex, energy intensive structures, and another for small, modest, owner-built houses: a "People's building code." Some counties in California already have such a thing, sometimes referred to as an "owner-builder code." In the absence of such a code, there are still ways to practice earthen building methods within the existing regulatory framework.

2. Earthen buildings are not illegal
It is important to understand that the code does not "outlaw" building with earth. On the contrary, many codes contain language that encourages building officials to be open to new, environmentally friendly ways of building. However, because of liability concerns and lack of understanding, seldom will a building department approve things without the approval of a structural engineer, which can be a long and costly process.

Most building codes are local. Counties usually start with adopting the national (or

"International") code and then make changes as they see fit. For example, insulation codes are different in Buffalo, NY than they are in San Diego, CA.

The final authority usually lies with the inspector coming to the building site. This can be good and bad. You may have built according to a set of approved plans and still be rejected by the inspector; conversely, you may do things that seem reasonable but would never get approved by the plan reviewers, yet a friendly inspector may approve it on the site.

All these things suggest that building codes may not always be as rigid as they appear. Taking on the attitude that the codes and code officials are there to help, rather than hinder, will help you achieve more of your goals.

3. You can get most of what you want
Many earthen building methods don't even require the approval of an inspector. Earthen plasters can be applied on the inside and outside of most buildings, earthen floors are seldom a problem. Non-load bearing interior walls can be made of such things as cob (make sure the floor is strong enough) or light-straw-clay. Outdoor rooms and patios can be shaped with walls made from cob, some form of earthen brick, or earthbags. When approaching the problem from this angle, it opens new and creative ways of thinking, by not defining a house solely by what holds up the roof, but rather by the sum of all the materials inside and out. This change of perspective can help us become aware of the fact that it's not just the code that is in the way: it's also the way we define houses. For example, I built a house where 2 x 4's hold up the roof, straw bales provide the insulation in the walls, cotton provides the insulation in the ceiling, earthen plasters and floors cover the inside, and interior cob "pony" walls shape interior spaces. Both inside and out, the house feels overwhelmingly like a "house of earth" and was easily accepted by the code officials. No one calls my house a "2 x 4 house," or a "cotton house," even though it is just that, as much as it would be a cob or a straw bale house.

In summary, the structural (load bearing) part of a house is only a small part of what creates the overall spirit of the house. By creatively integrating earthen materials into a more conventional building design, you can get a code approved earthen house!

4. Structure
It is still valuable to take a closer look at the structural component of a house and how it applies to earthen construction. For all municipalities, except for the few that have an owner-builder code, the supporting structure of a house (the part that holds up the roof and prevents it from blowing away) needs to be engineered. The strength of materials made from local ingredients like earth and straw are difficult, if not impossible, for an engineer to calculate. It can theoretically be done, but could require testing each individual batch of cob, and it would be very expensive.

Simple wood or metal framed walls can be easily designed to please the most conservative engineer, and at very little cost (the building industry has done all the work for you: the load-bearing capabilities of lumber and steel are very well known). This is especially true if you keep the shape of your building simple (a very good idea!). Once the "skeleton" is approved, you can fill it in with your choice of building materials. That is more or less how most straw bale houses and light straw-clay houses are built: the support members are not actually the straw bales, but rather a stud or timber frame structure.

5. Insulation

Most counties have strict rules with regards to the amount insulation required in the walls and ceilings. An earthen wall would have to be over 2 feet thick in order to comply with many of these standards. While a 2′ earthen wall would be fine (and even architecturally appealing), it's a lot of work and not necessary. Through a simple calculation, you can compensate for lack of insulation in the walls by adding more insulation in the ceiling. Since warm air rises and mostly wants to get out through the ceiling, putting extra insulation in the ceiling makes a lot of sense. The building code actually provides a calculation you can do yourself, which can then convince building officials to let you have a little less insulation in the walls.

Insulation value is expressed in R-value. The greater the R-value of a material, the more slowly heat (or cold) will travel through that material. In areas that have cold winters, or very hot summers, a minimum R-value of 19 in the walls and 38 in the ceiling is typically required. A 18 inch earthen wall has an R-value of about 10, not enough for the code.

Here is how the calculation works:

Let's say that the total square footage of your walls (minus doors and windows) equals 1000. If you multiply that by 19, that would give you the number of "insulation points" the code requires you to have, in our example that would be 19,000.

However, you are planning to build with earth and only will have a wall with an R-value of 10. This would give you 10,000 point. You are thus 9,000 points short. Now, let's say your ceiling is 700 square feet. The required R-value is 38, which would give you 38×700=26,600 points. If you were to increase your ceiling insulation by a little more than 1/3, you would gain the 9,000 points you are lacking in your walls.

This is relatively easy to do and would also make a lot of sense in terms of creating a comfortable building envelope. You would actually end up up with a better insulated building because increased ceiling insulation is more effective than increased wall insulation (heat rises).

6. The "200 square foot" rule

Many counties allow people to build small structures without needing building permit. Sometimes the maximum size is 200 square feet, sometimes less. Sometimes they measure the inside floor space, sometimes the whole footprint of the building. There are also often height restrictions. Check with your local department to find out what the specifics of this rule are.

However, please remember: These small structures are meant to be auxiliary buildings to existing, permitted structures. If you put plumbing and electric in it, you still need to get separate plumbing and electrical permits for those features. According to the building department, these are under no circumstances considered "livable structures;" you cannot legally sleep or live in them. If you spend the night in one you are by law "camping" on your own land, which is often only allowed for a limited number of weeks per year. The "200 square foot rule" is meant for storage sheds, barns, etc, not for permanent living. But with a small water jug and sink, some LED lights and a camping stove, you can carve out a nice "cottage lifestyle" without causing too much suspicion. It is not practical for the building department to come and check to see how many nights you are camping in your small cottage. And if for some reason they do come out and order you to stop living there, as long as the building is under the maximum size for a non-permitted structure, they can't make you take it down. Once the code enforcers have left, you may even consider quietly moving back in!

2.9 Clay paints

Visit www.HouseAlive.org *for pictures and videos on this chapter.*

Clay based paints are different from earthen plasters in that they are a thin, cosmetic layer that sits on top of a smooth surface. A plaster is thicker, with the color embedded in it, while paints are more of a surface coloring. Plasters tend to have more depth and richness to them than paints. Nevertheless, sometimes paint may come in handy or can create a desired effect.

Compared to commercial paint, clay paints are
- Much softer and less durable.
- They are non-toxic and much easier to work with.
- They are completely breathable: water vapor will easily move through the layer of paint.
- And they are very easy to make yourself at a fraction of the cost of commercial paints.

Making a mural
on a plastered wall
Using just pigment
And water

Clay paints can be directly applied to earthen plasters, drywall, wood and concrete. They work well to soften up the color in a bedroom, living room or ceiling. It's best to avoid using them on surfaces that get a lot of exposure to water, such as bathrooms.

The basic recipe for clay paint is to mix dry finely screened (or purchased bagged) clay with flour paste in a 50/50 ratio, and add water to get the consistency you want. You can add iron oxide pigments to create a variety of colors. You can also put in other additives for texture and aesthetic effect, such as fine sand, finely screened straw, or mica flakes. Anything is fair game! Experiment. A little bit of linseed oil can improve the durability of the paint. Try one half cup per four gallons of paint.

Painting

Apply the paint as you would a commercial paint, using a brush or rollers. It is important to apply the clay paint in thin coats. At first it seems like there is nothing going on the wall, and the temptation is to put it on thicker. Doing so can make the paint too thick and crack later on. Put it on in a thin coat and let it dry. The color will start to appear as it dries. Usually a second coat will be desired; add additional coats for deeper color saturation.

You can also paint over earthen finish plasters with a mix of iron-oxide pigment, water and flour paste, called a color wash. The paint will be drawn into the earthen plaster a little, like a stain does on wood, to create a fresco effect. Even a thin solution of water and iron oxide pigment can be applied to a plastered wall. It is easy to make these paints. Experiment and make test batches.

Appendix

3.1 Foundations for heavy buildings

Visit www.HouseAlive.org *for pictures and videos on this chapter.*

Cob, earthen block, and earthbag walls make for very heavy buildings. They need to be sitting on the earth, which is very different from a lot of conventional buildings; they often are constructed on a wooden floor, hovering 18 inches above the earth. It's important to ensure the building is on stable ground without uneven settling or movement from groundwater or frost. A foundation for heavy buildings is made from two parts, a rubble trench and a stem wall.

The rubble trench

A rubble trench is a trench dug in the ground underneath where you want the walls to go and then filled with drainage rock or "rubble."

- The trench is typically between one and two feet deep (deeper in wetter climates or softer subsoil). The bottom of the trench slopes to a low point where a pipe will continue downhill away from the foundation until it hits "daylight" (the pipe emerges from the ground out the side of the hill). The idea is that any water that gets into the trench will flow out of the trench. A slope of a ¼" per foot is adequate to facilitate drainage.
- (Option) If it is not possible for the exit pipe to reach "daylight" (because your building site is level), you can end it in a constructed dry-well. Dig a hole about four feet wide and six feet deep (the larger the better) at least 20 feet from the foundation. Lead the exit pipe into the hole.
- Line the rubble trench with landscape cloth (available at garden supply stores) or something similar. This cloth will keep the trench from filling with silt or sand but will allow water to freely move in and out of the trench.
- On the bottom of the trench, place large, chunky rocks, four to six inches wide. There should be lots of spaces between the rocks so that water can flow easily through the bottom of the trench. You can also put in a perforated 3 or 4-inch drainage pipe and connect that to the pipe leaving the trench.
- Fill the rest of the trench to the top (and dry-well, if applicable) with round river rocks, one to two inches in diameter. You can also use broken glass, crushed or angular rock, or anything else that will drain water well.

This rubble trench will do the following for your building:

- It ensures that the building will not settle unevenly. Two feet underground, the earth is usually more constant than on the surface. The rocks will help spread out the weight evenly throughout the bottom and sides of the trench.
- When water is in the trench, usually because of heavy rain, it has an easy exit and will not make the ground below the building soggy.
- Because there is no standing water below the building, there is less of a chance of frost heave. This occurs when buildings shift because frozen water below them expands to a point where it actually lifts up the building, usually unevenly.
- For earthquake protection the building is on a nonrigid foundation, allowing it to move with the rocks that it sits on. In mild earthquakes the rubble may shift before the building does.

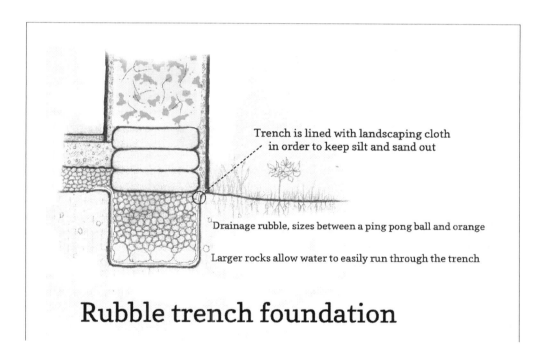

Trench is lined with landscaping cloth in order to keep silt and sand out

Drainage rubble, sizes between a ping pong ball and orange

Larger rocks allow water to easily run through the trench

Rubble trench foundation

The stem wall

The stem wall is the part of the foundation that is built up from the top of the rubble trench. Its function is to protect the walls from any moisture resulting from contact with the ground or flooding. It can be as low as one foot and as high as three feet. It is essential that earthen walls are protected from becoming saturated with water, due to a wet ground or flooding. A high stem wall, in combination with an overhanging roof, will also better protect the walls from sideways rain.

There are various options for the materials used to build a stem wall:

- Stone: stem walls built from stones can be beautiful. Make sure your stones you work with are large and have at least two mostly parallel sides. Otherwise, the stones are too difficult to build with. First "dry-stack" the stones without mortar and stabilize them with small stones (called "chinking") so they do not wobble. You should be able to walk on the wall without it feeling shaky. Then you can use cement or cob mortar to fill in the spaces. Inset the mortar a little for a visual effect; it makes the rocks stand out.
- Concrete: A poured concrete foundation with rebar inside it makes for a very strong foundation. Be aware though that concrete, through capillary action, can wick water from the ground up toward the earthen wall. Because of this, when you pour your foundation and the concrete is still wet, put lots of rocks in the very top, so that the cob will not directly touch the concrete. This will also create some teeth for the cob to connect to.
- Earthbags: This technique works very well for stem walls. It's not a bad idea to stabilize them with a little cement so that the earth inside the bags will remain solid, even if the bags get wet or disintegrate in the sun. (This shouldn't happen: be sure to plaster the bags to protect them from the sun!)
- Urbanite: This word describes chunks of concrete that can be found as a waste product in any urban environment. It's best to find pieces that are large, have no rebar in them, and have similar thicknesses. Broken up sidewalks or driveways are good sources of urbanite. Stack the urbanite like bricks, avoiding vertical seams. A layer of urbanite under an earthbag stem wall is also recommended.

Before constructing the rubble trench and the stem wall, think about any pipes, cables, or wires that will enter the house. In cold climates the water needs to come in below the frost line (level below which the ground never freezes), which in some areas can be well below the bottom of the rubble trench. It's possible to put sleeves (pieces of large diameter pipe as long as the width of the stem wall) in the stem wall, through which you can later put whatever wires and pipes you think you'll need. The leftover space in the sleeve can be filled with any combination of straw and cob.

3.2 Earthen Ovens

Visit www.HouseAlive.org *for pictures and videos on this chapter.*

Earthen ovens can be made almost entirely out of sand, straw, and clay-soil. They can be used to cook anything that can be cooked in a regular oven, but are best known for making outstanding bread and pizza. Because the inner layer is massive and continues to radiate heat after the fire is gone, you can cook different dishes as it slowly cools off: first pizza, then bread, then a cake, followed by drying fruit and herbs, perhaps yogurt, and finally, drying firewood for the next firing. A well-prepared person can make use of all the BTU's stored in the mass of the oven.

The shell of the earthen oven described here consist of four layers:
- a five-inch thermal layer made out of sand and clay-soil,
- a five-inch insulation layer made out of light straw-clay,
- a cap made out of straw-clay plaster,
- and a finish earthen plaster.

Almost all of the earthen building techniques described in this book can be applied to building an oven. It's a great community project that can be accomplished over the course of a weekend.

The foundation

It is best if the floor of the oven is at least two feet high. This makes it easier to tend the fire as well as the food. A basic oven has about a two-foot interior diameter, and the shell is about a foot thick. You will need a foundation that is about a four-foot diameter circle.

The first foot of foundation can be made out of urbanite, stone, or earthbags to keep the oven from wicking moisture from the ground. Thereafter, you can continue using the same material or switch to cob. You don't need to make the whole foundation solid: with smaller earthbags or rocks, you can build the outside circle and then fill and tamp the middle with whatever junk, rocks, or earth you have lying around.

The last six inches leading up to what will be the height of the oven floor consist of a one-foot wide ring of cob. Once this ring is built, fill it up with about three inches of sand and then start building the floor out of fire brick. You can also use fired clay brick (less heat resistant) or cob (more likely to leave sand on the bottom of your pizza) for the floor. Either way, the floor of the oven should end up flush with the top of the cob ring.

Another variation is to install a layer of a more insulating material such as pumice rock or vermiculite, instead or in combination with the sand. This will make it harder for the heat to be drawn down into the foundation, and useful for people who want to use the oven on a daily basis as it will maintain a lot of the heat into the next day.

When laying the fire bricks, the sand should be level and smooth. Use a rubber mallet or wooden dowel to gently tap the bricks into place. Aim for about a two-foot circle of fire bricks. Also lay three fire bricks where you want the entrance to be. You will have to cut out a space for these bricks in the cob circle. The whole two-foot circle does not need to be firebrick; odd corners can be filled with cob. This process may take some time. It is important that you try to minimize height differences between the bricks; keep them flush with each other so you can easily move food in and out of the oven.

Building the oven

Building the sand dome
The dome of the oven is more or less half of a sphere. To shape it you first make a form out of sand. With chalk draw a two- foot circle in the middle of the oven floor. Make a sand-dome on this circle about 18" high. Now you are essentially making a sand castle. For this to work well, it helps to wet the sand with clay-water, made by

Sand form is in place. Thermal layer is ready to be built

mixing two handfuls of clay-soil in a bucket of water. Sometimes the dome collapses a bit while building. That's OK; just keep trying. Do not pat the dome as this essentially

134

translates into mini-earthquakes for the dome. Use a machete or a sharp tool to shape the dome as needed. Ensure that the sides go up vertically for the first 8", making it easier to have firewood or food (loaves of bread) placed close to the sides.

Once you have a nice sand sphere, with 8" vertical sides and about 18" high, cover it with two layers of wet newspaper. This will make it possible to later on separate the sand from the thermal cob layer.

Building the thermal layer

This layer is about 4" or 5" thick and made out of a mixture of sand and clay-soil. It can have a little less clay-soil than cob because a sphere has a lot of structural integrity. By making it a little sandier, there will be less chance of cracking, even under high heat. You can mix the sand and clay-soil the same way you mix cob. Make sure to keep this mix pretty dry; because it lacks straw (which would burn), it will slump if it gets too wet.

As you are building the dome, use your hand as a guide for the thickness of this layer. It should be a little wider than the average palm. Build with the palm of your hand perpendicular to the curve of the dome. This way you can avoid pressing too much into the sand dome and can maintain the same thickness throughout the thermal layer. Use your other hand as a "moveable form."

Build up the thermal layer until there is only a small circle left on top of the dome, about a foot across. Add fresh material into this space and gently integrate it with the rest. To ensure you stick to a uniform thickness, put a small twig in the top of the sand dome and mark it where you want to build up to. Once you have reached this point, pull out the twig and fill the hole it created.

Cutting the door opening and taking out the sand

The thermal layer needs to dry somewhat before you can cut the opening for the door. You don't want it to dry completely, however, or it will be hard to cut. In warm summer months, with some wind, this could take about 24 hours. Aiming fans at the dome will greatly speed the drying process.

Once you think the dome has set up enough, use a machete or knife to cut the door opening about 12 inches high and between 12 and 15 inches wide, depending on what size pizza or pot you want to put in the oven. The 12-inch height of the opening is essential. It is just the right size to allow air to enter the oven through the bottom of the opening while the smoke exits the top. If you build a larger oven, always make sure the door is 2/3 the height of the inside of the dome.

With your hands or a small trowel, take the sand out of the dome, being careful not to damage the thermal layer. Don't worry about small pieces of paper left inside; they will burn off quickly once you start using the oven.

Shaping the door
While the thermal layer is still somewhat soft, it is easy to shape the entrance for a door. Scratch a line around the door opening, one inch in from the edge. Use a machete to make everything within this scratched line on the same flat plane. To test this, cut a piece of plywood into the shape of the entrance and hold it against the opening. There should be no spaces between the plywood and the oven. This piece of plywood can also become your door. If you cut that plane so that it is leaning into the dome at a slight angle, the door will stay shut simply by leaning into the oven a little bit, eliminating the need for hinges or other hardware. It will make it really easy to close the oven for baking. Wrap the plywood in aluminum foil so it doesn't catch on fire from the heat. You can also make a fancier door by adding some spacers and sheet metal on the inside face of the door.

The insulation layer
Before you put on the insulation layer, you will need to build a cob arch over the entrance; otherwise, the insulation will have no support over the door. Use cob that is sticky with a generous amount of straw in it. That will make it easier to form the arch. Shape the arch about 1 ½" away from the edge of the door so it will be easy to take the door in and out. Your oven now looks like a little igloo!

Pile a 5" layer of light straw-clay (made with plenty of clay slip) all over the dome. It should be easy to shape. If this layer does not have enough clay in it, the straw may actually start to smolder and burn when the oven gets really hot. Of course if you overdo the clay, the layer will lose insulation value and you will just be adding more mass to the dome. It should have enough clay in it so that it is easy to smooth out the insulation layer with your hands.

Finishing the oven
Cap the insulation layer with a layer of straw-clay plaster 2" to 3" thick. Once this layer is dry, which can take a day or two, you can add an optional earthen finish plaster to the oven. You can also choose to now make the oven a more interesting shape, using cob or straw-clay plaster to sculpt your oven into an animal, abstract art, a smoking dragon, etc.

Using the oven

During the first few uses, you may notice that the oven doesn't seem very hot or efficient. This is often due to the fact that the insulation layer is not totally dry; you essentially have an oven with a wet blanket around it. After a few uses the light straw-clay layer will have dried out.

To fire up the oven, start by building a small fire in the middle of the oven with paper and kindling. Once it is going, add some larger pieces of wood. Once it is burning well, use a hoe to push the whole fire carefully to the back of the oven. Continue to feed the fire in the back. This will cause the smoke to travel up over the ceiling of the dome and then down toward the door, heating up all the mass on the way. Once the oven gets quite hot, after about 20 minutes or so, you may notice that less or no smoke is coming out of the door. This is because the gases usually present in smoke are being burned off in the hot oven. If flames climb out of the door, your fire is too large. The flames inside should reach a little past the middle of the ceiling.

Over time you will learn how your oven performs. Each oven is a little different. Here are some guidelines to start with.

For bread baking:
- Fire the oven for about two hours.
- With a hoe or some other scraper, remove the coals and burning wood. A metal pan below the door is useful for this purpose.
- Use a stick with a wet rag attached to clean the area where you plan to put the bread. This size oven can accommodate about 5 or 6 loaves.
- Once the oven floor is clean enough, take a cup of water and throw in on the floor. It will steam up immediately, so be careful! Close the oven with the plywood door.
- Let the oven sit for about 15 minutes. This is called singing: the oven radiates heat in all directions, slowly equalizing the heat throughout. After this step, you can add another cup of water if you wish. The moisture is good for the bread baking process and it cools of the bricks a little so that the bottom of the bread won't burn. Put the bread in the oven, using a peel (like a large wooden spatula) to do so.

For pizza baking:
- Make a fire in the oven and let it burn for about 90 minutes.
- Move the fire to the side and back. If there's not much wood left, add some extra.
- Clean off the center of the oven with a wet rag on a stick.
- Make a pizza on a pizza peel and slide it onto the oven floor.

In the beginning the pizzas cook very fast, sometimes in less than a minute! The oven will slowly cool off, and after baking about 10 pizzas, you may need to build up the fire again for about 15 minutes. At this point it is okay to make the fire in the middle of the oven to increase the temperature of the floor.

If your oven is well built, you should be able to put your hand on the outside and hardly feel any heat, while the inside of the oven can be between 500 and 800 degrees. This high heat makes the crusts of the bread and pizzas so delicious.

Because the oven is made out of earth, it needs to be protected from the rain. You can make a simple oven umbrella by cutting some ribs out of plywood and covering them with plastic sheeting or canvas. You can also build a permanent roof over it, which is handy when it rains during a pizza party. Make sure that there is enough space between the roof and the oven so that it won't catch on fire. To be really safe, you can use sheet metal and metal pipes for rafters above the oven.

This may be helpful…
Learning how to build with earth

Learning how to build with earth will give you the tools you need to house yourself in a very satisfying and comfortable way. You will be able to look at a wall, a floor, or a fireplace and say: "I built that, and just the way I wanted it." Building with earth is not very difficult and you don't have to become a "master builder" in order to do beautiful work. Here are the four things (in no particular order) that seem to have worked best for other people who want to develop these skills:

1. Take a workshop.
As with all skill building, it is best to spend some time with someone else who is good at what you want to learn. Not that you can't figure it all out by yourself, but doing so can be expensive, time consuming and sometimes dangerous. Many people take a workshop, as it is the most condensed way of learning practical skills. In 2 to 8 weeks, you can learn the basic skills needed to build a little cottage. Occasionally work-trade opportunity may arise, where you can build with someone on their project, in return for room and board as well as a learning experience.

2. Work in conventional construction.
If you want to build something larger than just a little hut or garden wall, having experience with conventional construction techniques can be really helpful. You will learn a lot about structural requirements and building with wood, as well as how to install plumbing, electric, and windows and doors. You will learn how to swing a hammer and use a cordless drill. Furthermore you can experience first-hand how loud, dangerous, wasteful and unhealthy a conventional construction site can be and thus gain extra motivation to do things differently.

3. Broaden your vision.
Every teacher and builder will have their own way of doing things. Their style is the result of years of experience and is shaped by who they are as a person. You can learn from them, appreciate what they do, but not necessarily want to build and work the way they do. Visit a variety of building sites and meet as many builders as you can. Read books and browse the Internet, not to find the one and only method, but more to help you get in touch with who you will be as a builder. Become a "fusion builder," combining the best of what you find.

4. Start building close to the edge of your comfort zone.
This means taking on projects that are challenging and interesting enough to create an exciting learning curve for yourself, but that are not so difficult that they set you up for disappointment, failure or disaster. Needless to say this "edge" is different for all people, depending on their previous building experience, sense of adventure, strength, available tools, materials, and resources. It is very common (in any style of

construction) that people "bite off more than they can chew" and then get burned out, injured, divorced, or squeezed financially. IT IS NOT WORTH IT! Start small, take your time.

Here is another way to look at your learning process: a good builder knows a great number of "tricks" that make their work easier and better. This may include anything from how to pull a nail out of a piece of wood, to knowing how to carve a niche into an earthen wall. Non-builders may already have 100 tricks available. During a good workshop, you could acquire 1500 more tricks, allowing you to start experimenting with some projects. Once you develop your skills and explore building through other builders and projects, you will learn many more tricks, maybe up to to 3 or 4 thousand. As time goes on, the learning process slows down, since you've learned all the "easy stuff." You'll spend more time refining what you already know, and occasionally adding something new. Eventually, you may call yourself a master-builder, with as many as 10,000 tricks. Not many people get there; most of us land at the 4000 level, feeling confident that we can house ourselves in a beautiful and healthy way.

About the author:

Conrad Rogue has been teaching earthen construction for the past 15 years. His structures can be found in the United States, Mexico, India, Spain and Italy. He lives in a small cob cabin (Picture). If he is not building with mud, he is most likely playing guitar or drinking a glass of wine with friends. Or both!

Printed in Poland
by Amazon Fulfillment
Poland Sp. z o.o., Wrocław

52571553R00081